CLOSE AIR SUPPORT
ARMED HELICOPTERS & GROUND ATTACK AIRCRAFT

F-18E

GREENHILL MILITARY MANUALS

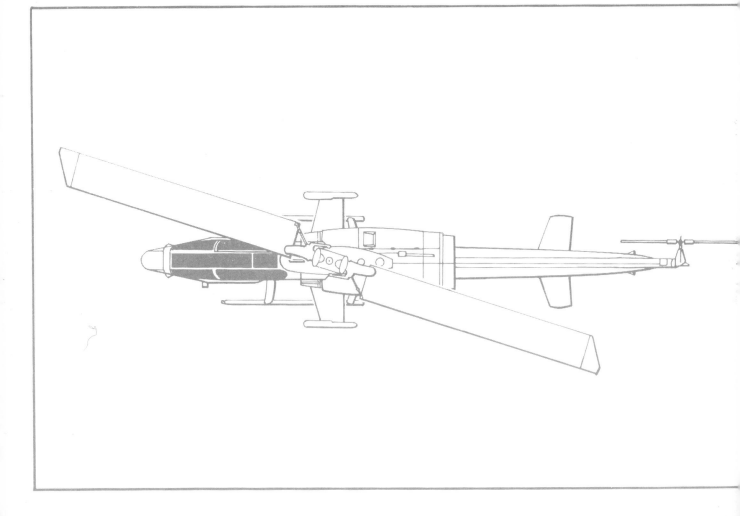

CLOSE AIR SUPPORT
ARMED HELICOPTERS & GROUND ATTACK AIRCRAFT

GREENHILL MILITARY MANUALS

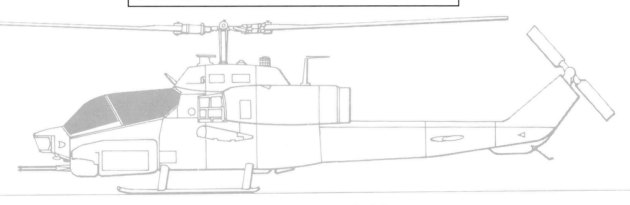

MICHAEL J. H. TAYLOR
ILLUSTRATED BY RAY HUTCHINS

Greenhill Books, London
Stackpole Books, Pennsylvania

Close Air Support: Armed Helicopters and Ground Attack Aircraft
first published 1996 by
Greenhill Books, Lionel Leventhal Limited, Park House
1, Russell Gardens, London NW11 9NN
and
Stackpole Books, 5067 Ritter Road, Mechanicsburg, PA 17055, USA

British Library Cataloguing in Publication Data
Taylor, Michael J. H. (Michael John Haddrick), 1949-
Close air support : armed helicopters and ground attack aircraft
- (Greenhill Military Manuals; No. 7)
1. Close air support 2. Attack planes 3. Attack helicopters
I. Title II. Series III. Hutchins, Ray 358.4' 142
ISBN 1-85367-240-8

Library of Congress Cataloging in Publication Data
Taylor, Michael John Haddrick.
Close air support : armed helicopters and ground attack aircraft/
by Michael J. H. Taylor, illustrated by Ray Hutchins.
144p. 15cm - - (Greenhill Military Manuals)
ISBN 1-85367-240-8
1. Close air support-- Handbooks, manuals, etc. 2 Attack planes-- Handbooks, manuals etc.
3. Attack helicopters--Handbooks, manuals etc.
I Title. II. Series.
UG 700.T39 1996
358 . 4' 142-- dc20   95 - 26431
CIP

Typeset by Vector Publicity and Communications
Printed and bound in Great Britain by
The Bath Press, Avon

Introduction

Close air support is the generic term for combat aeroplanes and helicopters used in several ways at the front line of battle. They add air-launched firepower to that of friendly ground forces in co-ordinated actions to assist movement and suppress the enemy, and they also attack enemy targets directly implicated in the battle. Less widely known but closely related is the task of battlefield air interdiction, intended to hamper enemy movement behind the front line and thereby severely restrict the chances of enemy reinforcements reaching the battle.

Waves of Allied Hawker Typhoon fighter-bombers ranging across the invasion theatre and wreaking havoc on Axis armoured vehicles during 1944-45 proved once and for all the devastating effect air power could have on the ground battle situation. It is unquestionable that such air attacks with 20 mm cannon and rockets or bombs greatly assisted the break-through to the Rhine and played a part in bringing a speedy peace to a war-weary Europe.

In our present decade, the massive deployment of air power in the Middle East in the early 1990s for a mainly ground attack role was instrumental in rendering ineffective one of the world's largest land armies, when coalition air forces flew more than 110,000 sorties in just 43 days.

Most armed aircraft can undertake close air support and battlefeld air interdiction, but it has been the widespread deployment of "smart" weapons that has had the greatest effect on modern military planning, allowing devastating attack with pinpoint accuracy and thereby avoiding casualties to both close-in friendly forces and non-combatants. Of course, more conventional bombs, rockets and guns are still relied upon in many instances.

The Vietnam conflict brought about the first use of specially-designed attack helicopters, soon gaining proven anti-armour credentials. Since sprouting masses of optical and electronic wizardry, together with their ability to fly nap-of-the-earth (hugging the ground) at high speed and wage combat at night, modern attack helicopters have become even more hard hitting and amongst the most difficult to defeat. Their capability to "live" with moving ground forces (requiring no runway) and therefore always be on instant call is shared by only one family of fixed-wing aeroplanes, the Harriers.

5

Contents

The Future

Most of the combat aircraft that will be in service well into the next century are known, though some are yet to fly. This inescapable fact reflects the years of design, development and testing needed before production and then operational flying can begin. India's Light Combat Aircraft, China's Chengdu FC-1 and J-10, and Russia's Mikoyan 1-42 will all probably fly in 1996, while already flown as prototypes are the European Eurofighter 2000, French Dassault Rafale and US Lockheed Martin F-22, to name a few. And whilst ground attack might not be the principal role for these, all are capable of such missions and will be so employed as required. In the case of the F-22, this important secondary task was added as an afterthought. A future warplane developed specifically for close air support and other attack roles is Japan's Mitsubishi FS-X, though, having been rolled out as a prototype in 1995, it will still not see service until the turn of the century. Another Japanese company, Kawasaki, is developing the nation's first indigenous tandem two-seat armed helicopter. Propeller-driven aircraft are not overlooked either, with Brazil's Embraer Super Tucano turboprop trainer having a new anti-guerrilla and attack role in ALX form.

The least known of the forthcoming combat types are the Mikoyan 1-42 and Chengdu J-10, the MiG having been expected to fly in 1995 but with no indication that it happened. The J-10 was the subject of much speculation in late 1995, believed to be based strongly on Israel's abandoned Lavi and thereby raising the blood pressure of many US officials who view such technology transfer with suspicion.

Clearly, in a book of this size, it is impossible to detail all aircraft capable of ground attack. Indeed, none of the futuristic types mentioned above are among the 53 main entries, not least because this book details aircraft currently used for attack or about to be, although an exception has been made in the case of the Boeing Sikorsky RAH-66 Comanche.

So, what of the future? The introduction mentioned "smart" weapons, and these include laser guided. The more widespread use of lasers is without question at the forefront of warfare technology, along with engine thrust vectoring that allows conventional warplanes to take-off in much shorter distances and have greater manoeuvrability. F-22 has thrust vectoring, as does the new Russian Sukhoi Su-35, though the Harriers still stand alone in their ability to fly vertically and backwards and make use of clearings instead of longer airstrips.

A unique concept in the USA has been to start development of the X-32, intended to be offered in both conventional and vertical landing forms, each with thrust vectoring but the latter with an additional "lift fan" mounted horizontally aft of the cockpit. And in what is probably among the greatest indicators for the future, Russia's Yakovlev organization has been invited to contribute its experience to the American programme.

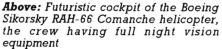

Above: *Futuristic cockpit of the Boeing Sikorsky RAH-66 Comanche helicopter, the crew having full night vision equipment*

Above Right: *86% representation of Lockheed Martin's X-32B, with a lift fan aft of the cockpit. A full-sized production version is viewed as a potential future replacement for Hornet, Harrier II and Sea Harrier*

Below Right: *A projected F-22 naval derivative strike/fighter with swing wings, the nearest of which is launching a GBU-24 guided bomb against enemy armour*

Aermacchi MB-339C　　　　　　　　　　　Italy

The **MB-339C** is the most powerful version of the MB-339 series, and carries the widest range of equipment to fulfil an expanded combat role. Head-up display (HUD) allows the pilot to be presented with vital information on a transparent plate at eye level, whilst an electronic display screen (CRT) has replaced some of the former instrumentation. **MB-339C** also has warning systems for self protection, chaff/flare to repel incoming missiles, and a laser rangefinder.

A wide range of attack weapons can be carried on six underwing pylons, with two pylons alternatively suited to carrying drop tanks to offer extra fuel for increased range. Weapons can include 7.62 mm or 12.7 mm machine gun or 30 mm cannon pods, rocket launchers, bombs of various types, Maverick air-to-surface or Marte Mk 2A anti-shipping missiles, and even Sidewinder or Magic air-to-air missiles for self-defence and air engagement. The aircraft's single Rolls-Royce Viper 680-43 turbojet engine provides 19.39 kN thrust.

Besides attack, the **MB-339C**'s roles include advanced and fighter lead-in training, with the instructor seated behind the trainee in a separate tandem cockpit, occupying a raised ejection seat to provide good forward vision. Indeed, the MB-339 was originally conceived principally for training, first flying as a prototype in 1976 and with large numbers of MB-339As entering Italian Air Force service from 1978 as advanced trainers plus other uses including radio calibration and aerobatic display team flying. From late 1996, the Italian Air Force is to receive MB-339CDs, based on the MB-339C but including new digital avionics. A more dedicated anti-shipping version of MB-339 has been developed as the MB-339AM, which has introduced radar to the aircraft. The very latest version is the MB-339FD, a fully digital model proposed to meet a Royal Australian Air Force requirement. Other users of MB-339s are Argentina (navy), Dubai, Ghana, Malaysia, Nigeria and Peru, but with New Zealand as the sole operator of the MB-339C in early 1996.

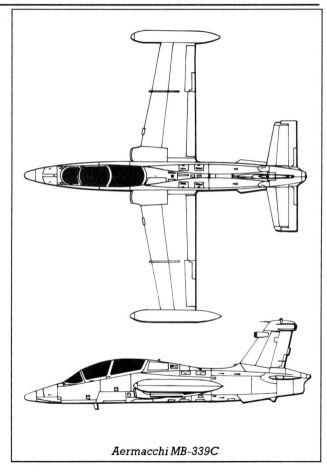

Aermacchi MB-339C

Specification

First prototype: 17 December 1985
Current users: New Zealand
Crew: Two
Wing span: 11.22 m
Length: 11.24 m
Height: 3.994 m
Empty weight: 3,430 kg
Max take-off weight: 6,350 kg
Max weapon load: 1,815 kg
Maximum speed: 900 km/h
Maximum rate of climb: 2,160 m per minute at sea level
Service ceiling: 14,240 m at sea level
Maximum range: 2,037 km for non-combat ferry flight, when using two 325 litre drop tanks

MB-339C flying in wintry conditions.

Aero L-39, L-59, L-139 and L-159   Czech Republic

First flown in 1968, the tandem two-seat **L-39** (Albatros) achieved widespread acceptance as a simple but strong training aircraft, of which 2,094 of over 2,800 built went to the Soviet/Russian/CIS forces in L-39C training form. Of several derivative versions produced, the **L-39ZO** is noteworthy for having strengthened wings with four (instead of 2) underwing pylons, making it adaptable for light attack.

L-39ZOs serve with Germany (inherited from East Germany), Iraq, Libya, Syria and Vietnam. As with the **L-39ZA**, power is provided by a 16.87 kN Ivchenko PROGRESS AI-25TL turbofan engine, and weapon load is similar. But **L-39ZA** is the recognised attack and reconnaissance version, and has the addition of an underfuselage gun pod. A multi-purpose version of ZA is the **L-39ZA/MP**, featuring Western avionics that include a HUD.

L-59 appeared in 1986 as a more capable aircraft, adding shore defence, counter-insurgency and air defence to the usual training and light attack roles. Powered by a 21.58 kN Ivchenko PROGRESS DV-2 turbofan, it has an 875 km/h top speed and a 1,500 kg pylon load. Users are the Czech Republic, Egypt and Tunisia.

L-139 (Albatros 2000) (first flown in 1993) is a development of the **L-39** which uses American avionics and engine, the latter an 18.15 kN AlliedSignal TFE731-4-1T turbofan, offering a 760 km/h top speed, while **L-159** is a more dedicated combat variant of the **L-59**, with accommodation for a pilot only. Using a 28.02 kN AlliedSignal/ITEC F124-GA-100 turbofan engine, **L-159** will first fly in 1996 and is expected to have a 930 km/h top speed at sea level and carry up to 2,340 kg of weapons for close air support, counter-insurgency, anti-shipping, air defence, or weapon/fighter lead-in training roles.

The **L-159** is be operated initially by the Czech Republic.

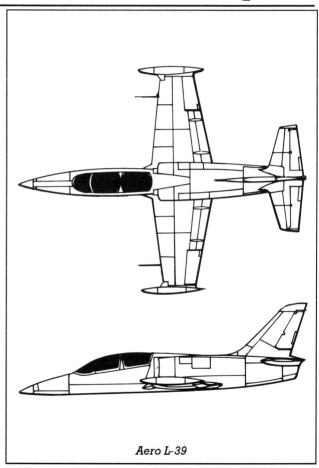

Aero L-39

Specification (L-39ZA)

First prototype: 29 September 1976
Current users: Algeria, Bulgaria, Czech
Republic, Nigeria, Romania, Slovakia,
Syria, Thailand and Vietnam
Crew: Two
Wing span: 9.46 m
Length: 12.13 m
Height: 4.77 m
Empty weight: 3,565 kg

Max take-off weight: 5,600 kg
Max weapon load: 1,290 kg
Maximum speed: 630 km/h
Maximum rate of climb: 810 m per
minute at sea level
Service ceiling: 7,500 m
Maximum range: 1,800 km for L-39C (as a
guide), with drop tanks

*L-59 with underfuselage cannon and
underwing bombs.*

Agusta A 109CM, K2 and KM   Italy

First flown in 1971, the **A 109** is both a civil and military multi-purpose helicopter that has been developed over the years into a series of six versions plus sub-variants, with three engine choices.

It is currently serving with the armed forces of ten countries, plus many civil, emergency medical service and para-military operators. Military versions are the **A 109CM, K2** and **KM**, though the K2 is equally at home in special non-military and law enforcement forms.

The **A 109CM** is a military variant of the civil A 109C, using two similar 336 kW Allison 250-C20R/1 turboshafts and a 4-blade composites-built main rotor. It is usually equipped with an advanced mission package that includes a cockpit management system for the control and integration of the communications, navigation and data transfer sub-systems.

Possible uses are many, but for anti-tank, scouting, light attack, escort and area suppression it can be equipped with the HeliTOW anti-tank missile system for launching TOW 2As, or alternative 12.7 mm or 7.62 mm gun pods, or 70 or 81 mm rocket launchers, plus gyrostabilised sight, and FLIR and night vision goggles for night operations.

A wide range of survival equipment can include radar warning, infra-red jammer, chaff/flare dispenser, and armoured crew seats.

Users include the Belgian Army.

The **A 109K2** is the version particularly suited to operations in hot temperatures and at high altitudes, due to its two powerful 471 kW Turbomeca Arriel 1K1 turboshaft engines.

By developing the **A 109KM**, Agusta went one stage further, combining the K2's hot-and-high capabilities with the CM's comprehensive weapon and mission systems.

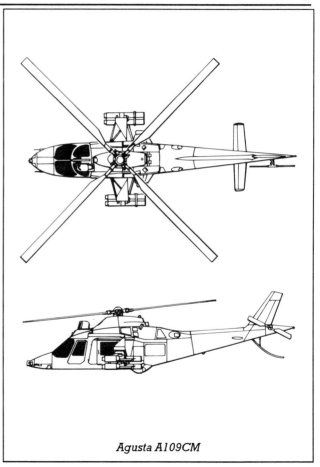

Agusta A109CM

14

Specification

First prototype: 1983 for the A 109K
Current users: See text
Crew: Pilot and up to 7 others
Main rotor diameter: 11 m
Length: 13.035 m with rotors turning
Height: 3.5 m
Empty weight: 1,650 kg
Max take-off weight: 3,000 kg with external load, 2,850 kg with internal load
Max weapon load: See text
Maximum cruise speed: 265 km/h for KM
Maximum rate of climb: 618 m per minute at sea level for KM
Service ceiling: 6,100 m
Hovering ceiling in ground effect: 5,300 m for KM
Hovering ceiling out of ground effect: 3,900 m
Maximum range: 806 km for KM, with auxiliary tanks

A 109CM fitted with anti-tank missiles.

Agusta A 129 Mangusta Italy

The **Mangusta** is one of the most advanced specialised combat helicopters in service in Western Europe, suited to anti-tank, escort and armed scout, air support and air-to-air combat. It was designed to be hard hitting and to have complete ballistic tolerance to strikes from enemy 12.7 mm ground fire, while also capable of surviving 23 mm hits. Layout is of the classic tandem, height staggered and armour protected cockpit arrangement for the two crew, with features to ensure crew survival and minimum aircraft damage after an 11 metre per second crash impact that include pyrotechnic energy egress, roll-over bars and A-shaped reinforced frame, and energy absorbing undercarriage, seats, fuel cells and airframe.

Costing and weighing under half that of some other specialised attack helicopters currently on offer, **Mangusta** can nevertheless operate in all conditions, by day or night, due to its weapon systems, electro-optical equipment and infra-red sensors for combat and navigation, and even in nuclear/biological/chemical contaminated environments without the need for special protective suits for the crew.

Powered by two Rolls-Royce Mk 1004 turboshaft engines, each rated at 657 kW at take-off, the **Mangusta** carries its weapons on four pylons under the stub-wings. Choices include 8 TOW 2A or Hellfire anti-armour missiles, launchers for 68 mm, 70 mm or 81 mm rockets, 20 mm gun pods and even air-to-air missiles. Combinations can weigh up to 1,200 kg. The stub-wings themselves can be elevated or depressed to help weapon launching.

In early 1996 the Italian Army was the only operator, requiring 60 for attack and scouting roles, with deliveries still underway, 15 of which are being retrofitted with an undernose gun and Stinger air-to-air missiles.

A more powerful variant with standard undernose gun and upgraded avionics is the A 129 International, first flown on 9 January 1995 and also available for export.

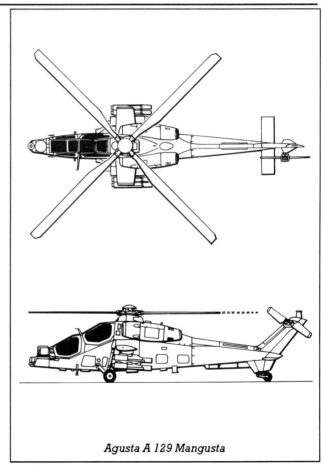

Agusta A 129 Mangusta

Specification

First prototype: 11 September 1983
Current users: Italian Army
Crew: Two
Main rotor diameter: 11.9 m
Length: 14.29 m with rotors turning
Height: 3.35 m
Empty weight: 2,529 kg
Max take-off weight: 4,100 kg
Max weapon load: 1,200 kg
Maximum speed: 275 km/h
Maximum rate of climb: 612 m per minute
Service ceiling: 4,725 m
Hovering ceiling in ground effect: 3,140 m
Hovering ceiling out of ground effect: 1,890 m
Maximum range: 561 km

A Mangusta A129 fitted with TOW 2A missiles

AMX International AMX

AMX is a light, high-subsonic close air support, battlefield interdiction and reconnaissance single-seater, developed and produced jointly by Embraer of Brazil and Aermacchi and Alenia of Italy. Its somewhat conventional appearance masks many very modern features, not least of which are head-up and head-down cockpit displays, two electronic flight computers and digital MIL STD 1553B databus, composite materials used in the construction on the tailfin and elevators, and a fly-by-wire system which controls the variable-incidence tailplane, rudder and spoilers. A combat-capable two-seat trainer variant is the AMX-T. Brazil requires 94 single/two-seaters (single-seaters known as A-1s in service), and Italy 238, though only about half have been ordered for the respective air forces, with service entry from 1989.

The aircraft for the two air forces are generally similar, though with some noteworthy differences that include SMA/Tecnasa Scipio multi-mode coherent radar and two 30 mm DEFA 554 cannon in Brazilian A-1s, and FIAR Grifo F/X multi-mode pulse-Doppler radar, one 20 mm M61A1 Vulcan multi-barrel cannon and a Thomson-CSF laser designator pod in Italian AMXs. Each aircraft is powered by a 49.1 kN Rolls-Royce Spey RB168-807 turbofan engine. Low vulnerability in a hostile environment was an early design goal, achieved partly by high performance at low level, but also through the use of active and passive electronic countermeasures, radar and missile warning systems, and chaff/flare dispensers.

Weapons can be carried on the underfuselage and four underwing pylons, up to 3,800 kg total weight, with two wingtip launch rails for Sidewinder, Piranha or Mol air-to-air missiles for self-defence or a counter-air role. Twin or triple carriers for the main pylons greatly increase the number of individual weapons that can be carried, while about ten Italian two-seaters were earmarked for modification to undertake an electronic combat role, each carrying anti-radiation missiles, jammer pod and other equipment.

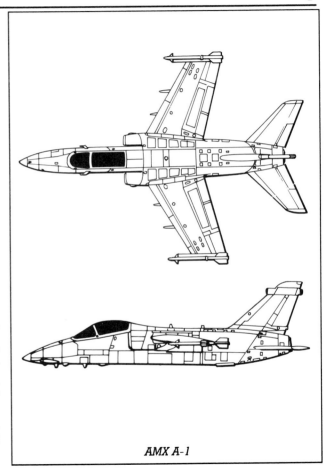

AMX A-1

Specification

First prototype: 15 May 1984
Current users: Brazil and Italy
Crew: Pilot only, or two in the AMX-T and electronic warfare versions
Wing span: 9.97 m over the wingtip missiles
Length: 13.23 m
Height: 4.55 m
Empty weight: 6,700 kg
Max take-off weight: 13,000 kg
Max weapon load: 3,800 kg
Maximum speed: Mach 0.86
Maximum rate of climb: 3,124 m per minute at sea level
Service ceiling: 13,000 m
Maximum range: 926 km radius of action

Italian AMXs with wingtip Sidewinders.

19

Atlas CSH-2 Rooivalk South Africa

Development of **Rooivalk** is a remarkable achievement for a nation that has a very small domestic requirement for a specialist attack helicopter and has to compete with many of the world's longest-established helicopter producers for international export orders. Yet, so capable and agile is this helicopter that it had been viewed at the outset as a very serious competitor in the competition to equip the British Army, not least because it is relatively inexpensive. However, although Britain eventually chose another system, to date 16 **Rooivalks** have been ordered for the South African Air Force, delivered from March 1996, for a single squadron.

This tandem two-seater, powered by two uprated Topaz turboshaft engines (derived from the French Turbomeca Makila 1A1) of 1,492 kW each at take-off, has considerable dynamic component commonality with the Puma transport helicopter, with the maintenance advantages that imparts. **Rooivalk** was designed to be capable of taking the tactical initiative and surviving the crucial first day of a conventional conflict, and was designed also to permit 90% of its long service life to be flown on nap-of-the-earth operations at a mere 5 to 20 metres altitude to enhance surprise and survivability. The state of the art integrated weapon system encompasses weapon and stores management via a stabilised turret with forward looking infra-red imaging and low light-level television, laser ranging and designation. Additionally, autotracking, crew helmet, head-up displays, and other features allow day and night operations in its principal roles of anti-tank, deep penetration, close air support, battlefield air interdiction, escort and reconnaissance.

Eight or sixteen anti-tank missiles can be carried on the four stub-wing pylons, with other choices including launchers for 44 or 88 rockets (68 mm), or a mix of both. Wingtip launchers provide positions for four air-to-air missiles. The undernose cannon has 400 or 700 rounds of 20 mm high-velocity ammunition.

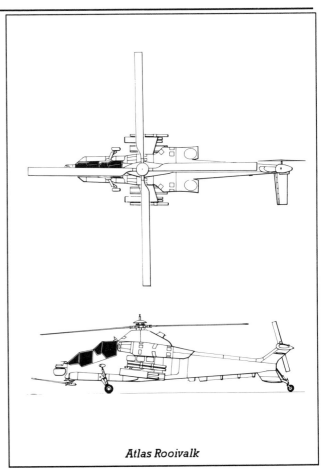

Atlas Rooivalk

Specification

First prototype: 11 February 1990
Current users: South African Air Force
Crew: Two
Main rotor diameter: 15.58 m
Length: 18.731 m, with rotors turning
Height: 5.187 m
Empty weight: 5,910 kg
Max take-off weight: 8,750 kg
Max weapon load: See text
Fast cruise speed: 278 km/h
Maximum rate of climb: 670 m per minute
Service ceiling: 6,100 m
Hovering ceiling in ground effect: 5,550 m
Hovering ceiling out of ground effect: 5,030 m
Maximum range: 700 km with internal fuel only

Foreground shows the Advanced Demonstration Model (ADM) of the CSH-2 Rooivalk with the XDM sporting the highly effective IR exhaust suppression system.

Avioane IAR-99 Soim   Romania

Soim was developed as a modern tandem two-seat advanced jet trainer, suited also to close air support when flown usually with only the pilot on board. It became yet another user of the British Rolls-Royce Viper turbojet engine, in this case the 17.66 kN Viper 632-41M built in Romania by Turbomecanica.

Instrumentation is conventional, and the weapon sight is of gyroscopic type.

It is believed that the Romanian Air Force has received about 50 **Soims**, and at least one other air force was reportedly in negotiation for export models in 1995.

The 23 mm GSh-23 cannon is housed in a detachable pod carried under the fuselage, with 200 rounds of ammunition, while 42 mm or 57 mm rocket launchers, pods for two 7.62 mm machine-guns, bombs of up to 250 kg weight or multi-store carriers can be attached to the four underwing pylons. As an alternative to weapons, two of the pylons are able to carry 225 litre drop tanks to extend range, though such carriage would normally indicate a combat mission and thereby would see the **Soim** mounting a mix of weapons and tanks.

With Israeli assistance, Avioane has also produced the prototypes of an upgraded and more combat-capable variant of **Soim** known as the IAR-109 Swift, featuring among many other changes a "glass" cockpit with modern head-up and head-down displays and TV monitor, plus laser ranger and much more, indicating the use of precision-guided bombs and missiles. Two air-to-air missiles remain another option for both aircraft types.

There is no indication as yet that Swift has been series built, or that in-service **Soims** have been upgraded to this standard.

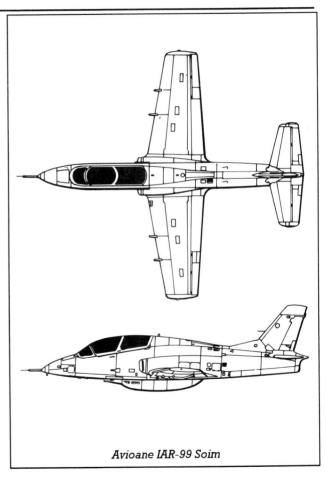

Avioane IAR-99 Soim

Specification

First prototype: 21 December 1985
Current users: Romania
Crew: Two, as instructor and trainee
(see text)
Wing span: 9.85 m
Length: 11.009 m
Height: 3.898 m
Empty weight: 3,200 kg

Max take-off weight: 5,560 kg
Max weapon load: 1,000 kg
Maximum speed: 865 km/h
Maximum rate of climb: 2,100 m per
minute at sea level
Service ceiling: 12,900 m
Maximum range: 1,100 km

*Romanian Air Force Soim with gun pod and
four rocket launchers awaiting take-off.*

Bell & Agusta-Bell 412EP Griffon   Canada/Italy

The US designed but Canadian built Bell **412EP** is basically a
15-place medium-size helicopter, powered by Pratt & Whitney
Canada PT6T-3D Twin Pac turboshafts with a combined rating of
1,342 kW at take-off. It has an advanced four-blade rotor system
permitting agile and high-speed performance which, when
viewed in combination with the rugged airframe and ballistic
tolerance of the dynamic components, provides for a highly useful
helicopter.

Although its usual roles are passenger and cargo transportation,
emergency medical services/medical evacuation (with 3
stretchers plus four ambulatory patients and two assistants or 6
stretchers and two assistants) and similar uses, it has gone into
substantial military service. One hundred have been ordered by
the Canadian Department of National Defence as CH-146 Griffons
for utility tactical transport and search and rescue.

412EP helicopters are also licence-built in Italy, and among the
available Italian sub-variants is a unique maritime patrol model
equipped with a forward-looking infra-red sensor (FLIR), a high-resolution
TV camera and 360° search radar among other specialised equipment.

However, as with Canadian production, the Agusta-Bell **AB412EP**
Griffon military model is capable of carrying substantial armament
if required for armed assault, close support, escort and other roles,
with optional weaponry including single or twin 7.62 mm guns in
pods, single 12.7 mm gun pod, 50 mm, 70 mm or 81 mm air-to-ground
rocket launchers, a pintle-mounted 7.62/12.7 mm gun and more.

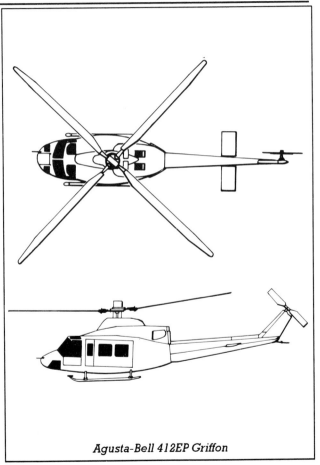

Agusta-Bell 412EP Griffon

Specification

Current users: Delivery of 412EPs to the Canadian Department of National Defence as CH-146 Griffons began in August 1994
Crew: See text
Main rotor diameter: 14 m
Length: 17.11 m with rotors turning
Height: 3.68 m
Empty weight: 2,914 kg
Max take-off weight: 5,398 kg

Max weapon load: See text
Cruise speed: 226 km/h
Maximum rate of climb: 542 m
Service ceiling: 5,395 m
Hovering ceiling in ground effect: 3,109 m
Hovering ceiling out of ground effect: 1,585 m
Maximum range: 745 km at 1,525 m

Canadian Forces CH-146 Griffon.

BAe and McDonnell Douglas Harriers

The original **Harrier** became the first fixed-wing V/STOL combat aircraft in the world to gain operational status, after entering service with the Royal Air Force in 1969.

Other users of the original **Harrier** were the US Marine Corps and the Spanish Navy. Indeed, Spain was the last to relinquish its aircraft, when Thailand took over remaining AV-8S Matadors (as they were known to Spain) in 1995, although some **Harrier** two-seat training variants remain with the original forces.

After early work on separate programmes, British Aerospace and McDonnell Douglas of the USA collaborated on a replacement design. Although this, the **Harrier II,** became greatly more formidable in the roles of close air support and interdiction, it was still widely based on the original **Harrier** concept but designed to offer double the payload or range. Features include lift improvement devices, new big wings with leading-edge root extensions, and much greater use of composites in airframe construction. Avionics were also upgraded, with RAF aircraft and later production AV-8Bs having forward-looking infra red sensors for night attack.

A non-afterburning Rolls-Royce Pegasus thrust-vectoring turbofan was again the power plant, though now with a small increase in thrust and, as before, having four rotatable nozzles mounted on the fuselage sides, able to swivel from fully aft for high speed horizontal flight through 98.5° for vertical and even backwards flight. The RAF version is the Pegasus 11 Mk 105, rated at 95.86 kN. Spanish EAV-8B Matador IIs were built with similarly rated Pegasus Mk 152-42s but these are being replaced by 105.89 kN Pegasus 11-61s, the engine type which, in F402-RR-408A form, powers USMC AV-8B models of **Harrier II** from the 167th model off the production line onwards. Earlier USMC AV-8Bs have the 95.42 kN Pegasus 11-21 (F402-RR-406A), as have the

Harrier GR. Mk 7

ex-USMC AV-8Bs used by the Italian Navy.

The weapon choice includes laser-guided precision bombs and air-to-surface missiles such as Maverick, plus Sidewinder or Magic air-to-air missiles.

All forces have some two seat trainers.

On 22nd September 1992 the **Harrier II Plus** first flew. Powered by the Pegasus 11-61/F402-RR-408, it introduced Hughes APG-65 multi-mode pulse-Doppler radar. The effect was to increase combat possibilities, not least in the use of AMRAAM for beyond-vision-range air-to-air engagement, plus the deployment of Harpoon and other missiles.

Harrier II Plus first joined the USMC in 1993, the Italian Navy in December 1994 and was ordered also by Spain.

It is likely that both Spain and the USA will also upgrade some earlier **Harrier IIs** to this standard.

RAF Harrier GR Mk 7 firing rockets.

Specification (Harrier II)

First prototype: 5 November 1981
Current users: See text
Crew: Pilot
Wing span: 9.25 m
Length: 14.35 m for the RAF's GR.Mk 7 and 14.12 m for the AV-8B
Height: 3.56 m
Empty weight: 6,831 kg for GR.Mk 7, and 6,337 kg for AV-8B
Max take-off weight: 13,494 kg for GR.Mk 7, and 14,061 kg for AV-8B
Max weapon load: 4,900 kg for GR.Mk 7, and 6,003 kg for high-powered AV-8B, both with short take-off run
Maximum speed: 1,083 km/h at sea level
Maximum range: 1,111 km radius of action for attack with two 1,000 lb bombs, 3 cluster bombs and two drop tanks

Above: A fully armed RAF Harrier GR Mk 7.

Opposite: A brace of fully armed Harrier II Plus on exercise.

British Aerospace Sea Harrier

Sea Harrier was developed during the 1970s as a ship-borne V/STOL multi-role aircraft for fleet air defence, strike, ship attack and reconnaissance. **Sea Harrier** first joined the Royal Navy in June 1979 as the FRS.Mk 1 for initial trials on board HMS Hermes.

In the following year trials were conducted on Hermes using the new "ski-jump" concept, whereby **Sea Harriers** could take off with a much heavier weapon and/or fuel load after a short deck run and jump from the upward-inclined ramp than was possible in a vertical take off. This led to the construction of ski-jumps on all three of the Invincible class carrier-cruisers that thereafter became home to the Royal Navy's sea-going **Sea Harriers**.

The Royal Navy received 57 **Sea Harrier FRS.Mk 1s** up to 1988, with about half that number seeing action during the Falklands conflict of 1982, when 2,380 sorties were flown and a large number of air victories were recorded. But limitations imposed by the original Blue Fox radar and Sidewinder air-to-air armament led to the development of the current F/A.Mk 2 version, which features much improved Blue Vixen multi-mode pulse-Doppler radar and deployment of AMRAAMs instead of, or as well as, Sidewinders. Indeed, F/A.Mk 2s were the first European combat aircraft to employ AMRAAMs. Twenty-nine FRS.Mk 1s were assigned for upgrade to F/A.Mk 2s, to be joined by 18 newly constructed aircraft.

The only other **Sea Harrier** operator is the Indian Navy, whose 19 remaining FRS.Mk 51s are receiving their own limited upgrade to keep them flying until the year 2010, when navalised HAL LCAs will replace them.

As with the land-based Harrier, **Sea Harrier** uses the thrust vectoring Rolls-Royce Pegasus turbofan engine for vertical lift and cruise flight, in this case the 95.64 kN thrust Pegasus 11 Mk 104

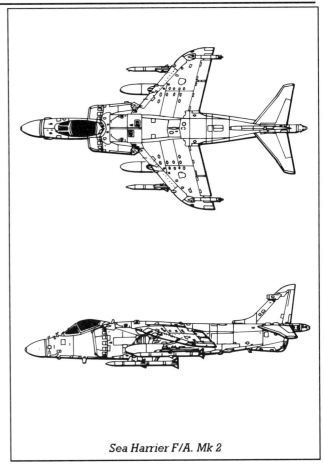

Sea Harrier F/A. Mk 2

or Mk 106.

Sea Harrier has four underwing pylons and three more possible positions under the fuselage, with weapon options for a ground attack, support and interdiction roles including free fall, cluster and retarded bombs, rockets and various missiles (including ALARM for attacking radar sites).

A nuclear weapon can also be carried in a strike role, but this capability is outside the scope of this book.

Two 30 mm Aden cannon pods can take the place of the normal strakes under the fuselage when required.

Indian Navy Sea Harrier FRS Mk 51 (Denis Hughes)

Specification
(FRS.Mk 1)

First prototype: 20 August 1978
Current users: India and the UK
Crew: Pilot
Wing span: 7.7 m
Length: 14.5 m
Height: 3.61 m
Empty weight: 6,298 kg
Max take-off weight: 11,884 kg
Max weapon load: 3,856 kg for short take-off, or 2,268 kg for vertical take-off
Maximum speed: 1,176 km/h at sea level
Maximum range: 463 km radius of action for attack

Above: A fully-armed Royal Navy Sea Harrier F/A Mk 2.

Opposite: Sea Harrier F/A Mk 2 leaving the ski-jump, carrying bombs and drop tanks in an attack configuration.

British Aerospace Hawk 50, 60 and 100

Hawk was originally developed as a high-subsonic advanced flying, navigation and weapons trainer for the Royal Air Force, to replace outdated Gnat and Hunter types. Delivery of 176 began in 1976 as Hawk T.Mk 1s, of which 88 were subsequently modified into T.Mk 1As to carry AIM-9L Sidewinder missiles when required for an emergency point air defence role or to fly missions alongside Tornados in a Mixed Fighter Force.

Hawk was designed to have four underwing pylons plus an underfuselage station for a gun pod or other store, although the two outer wing pylons had not been activated on the T.Mk 1. A Rolls-Royce Turbomeca Adour 851 turbofan engine was provided for the **Hawk Series 50**, the initial export model, of similar 23.31 kN rating to the RAF's Adour 151. Importantly, all five pylons were activated from the outset on the Series 50, indicating a greater emphasis on the secondary attack role, with up to a 2,721 kg load. Finland became the initial Series 50 operator, in 1980, whose Hawk Mk 51/51As differ from other Hawks in having a 12.7 mm gun instead of a 30 mm Aden cannon in the optional underfuselage pod.

The **Hawk Series 60** followed the **Series 50** to offer higher performance, due to its 25.4 kN Adour 861 engine. Weapon load increased to 3,000 kg and, like the **Series 50**, the inner wing pylons can carry drop fuel tanks. Avionics were upgraded, and a comprehensive stores management system included for its wider attack role.

Most significant from an attack standpoint was development of the **Hawk Series 100**, delivered from 1993. With a 26.65 kN Adour 871 engine, and new wings to improve lift and manoeuvrability plus wingtip launch rails for air-to-air missiles, this version can carry up to eleven individual weapons when using multi-store carriers (within the 3,000 kg total load limit). It also features head-up and head-down displays, a new weapon aiming computer and much else, plus the option of forward-looking infra-red and laser ranging sensors.

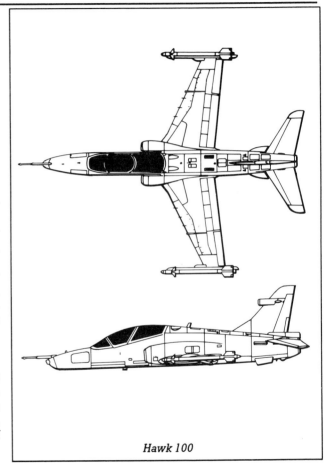

Hawk 100

Specification

First prototype: 21 August 1974 for the T.Mk 1

Current users: Abu Dhabi (Series 60 and 100), Dubai (Series 60), Finland (Series 50), Indonesia (Series 50 and 100), Kenya (Series 50), Kuwait (Series 60), Malaysia (Series 100), Oman (Series 100), Saudi Arabia (Series 60), Switzerland (Series 60), South Korea (Series 60), UK (T.Mk 1/1A) and Zimbabwe (Series 60)

Crew: Two, as instructor and trainee. Usually pilot only for combat roles

Wing span: 9.39 m

Length: 12.42 m for Series 60 and 100

Height: 3.99 m

Empty weight: 4,012 kg for Series 60, and 4,400 kg for Series 100

Max take-off weight: 9,100 kg for Series 60 and 100

Max weapon load: 3,000 kg for Series 60 and 100

Maximum speed: Mach 0.82 for Series 100

Service ceiling: 14,000 m for Series 60

Maximum range: 232 km typical radius of action for Series 100 in close air support role

Hawk 100 demonstrator.

British Aerospace Hawk 200

Hawk 200 was developed as a lightweight, multi-role single-seater to exploit and expand upon the full combat potential of the two-seat Hawk trainer for the export market. Based on the Hawk 100, and thereby having high-lift wings with leading-edge droop, full flap vanes, four flap positions with combat settings and wingtip missile rails, it was also given a nose-mounted Westinghouse APG-66H radar with ten air-to-surface and ten air-to-air modes.

Extra fuel tankage for the Adour 871 engine allows longer range, and an in-flight refuelling probe is optional. With two 591 litre drop tanks, **Hawk 200** can self-deploy over a distance of more than 2,500 km, a significant ability under emergency or mobilisation circumstances.

The number of weapon stations is the same as for the Hawk 100, and any of the four underwing pylons can carry a 907 kg load. A radar warning receiver and chaff/flare dispenser help survivability in a hostile environment.

Possible combat roles are many and varied, with close air support and battlefield air interdiction among the most important. However, **Hawk 200** is equally suited to air defence with four Sidewinders, cannon pod and drop tanks, maritime strike or support, and armed reconnaissance with cameras and infra-red linescan in a pod.

Non-combat uses can include target towing.

Oman became the first **Hawk 200** purchaser in 1990, with delivery of 12 from 1993. The two other operators at the time of writing were Indonesia with 16 and Malaysia with 18, while British Aerospace retains two for development and demonstrations.

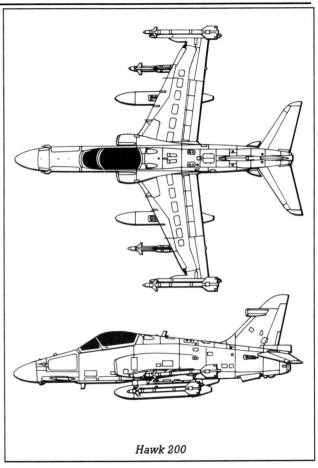

Hawk 200

Specification

First prototype: 19 May 1986
Current users: Indonesia, Malaysia and Oman
Crew: Pilot
Wing span: 9.94 m over wingtip missiles
Length: 11.35 m
Height: 4.14 m
Empty weight: 4,450 kg

Max take-off weight: 9,100 kg
Max weapon load: 3,000 kg typically
Maximum speed: 1,000 km/h at sea level
Maximum rate of climb: less than 7.5 minutes to climb to 9,150 m
Service ceiling: 13,500 m
Maximum range: See text

A fully armed Hawk 200 on patrol.

Bell Model 209 HueyCobra and SuperCobra

First flown on 7 September 1965, the **HueyCobra** was the result of Bell's revolutionary concept to produce a high-speed helicopter dedicated to attack, fire support, fire suppression and armed escort, without the normal passenger or cargo carrying cabin.

The fuselage was made extremely slim by placing the gunner and pilot in tandem, and the rear cockpit raised to provide suitable forward vision, resulting in a helicopter that presented an extremely small cross section to an enemy and was highly manoeuvrable and workmanlike, with armour protection. In addition to a chin gun turret, rockets and missiles could be carried under short stub-wings.

The original AH-1G **HueyCobra** very quickly proved its worth with the US Army in Vietnam and new models followed with even greater emphasis on the carriage of anti-armour missiles. Avionics were also enhanced at the time of manufacture or by retrofit, now allowing missile launch at night, in adverse weather, or through haze and dust.

Current operators of **HueyCobra** in various models are the US Army, Israel, Japan, Jordan, South Korea, Pakistan and Thailand, while in 1995 an agreement with Romania will see the production of 96 AH-1Fs by IAR at Brasov. The current principal AH-1F version is powered by a 1,342 kW AlliedSignal T53-L-703 turboshaft and is capable of 227 km/h.

Normal weapon load is 8 TOW missiles under outer stub-wing pylons, and rockets or up to 4 AAMs on the inner pylons.

In the early 1970s the US Marine Corps received a twin-engined version of **HueyCobra**, known as AH-1J SeaCobra, also supplied to Iran. An improved USMC version was the AH-1T, with upgraded engines and dynamic system. These are no longer in use with the USMC, but many AH-1Ts were converted into the

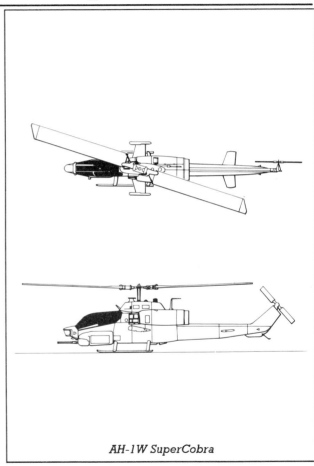

AH-1W SuperCobra

currently operated AH-1W **SuperCobra**, joining newly built examples. **SuperCobra** has two 1,212 kW General Electric T700-GE-401 turboshaft engines, and can now be retrofitted if wanted with a new 4-blade hingeless and bearingless main rotor (instead of two blade).

Weapon options can be 8 TOW II or Hellfire missiles, or a mix of both, 2.75 in or 5 in rockets, fuel air bombs, 20 mm gun pods, or other missiles of Maverick air-to-ground, AIM-9L Sidewinder air-to-air or Sidearm anti-radiation types.

Export customers are Taiwan and Turkey. During Operation Desert Storm, SuperCobras comprised under 20% of the attack helicopter force deployed, yet flew more than 50% of attack helicopter missions.

SuperCobra testing a performance-improving four-blade main rotor, under the designation AH-1W+4.

Specification (SuperCobra)

First prototype: 16 November 1983
Current users: See text
Crew: Two
Main rotor diameter: 14.63 m
Length: 17.68 m, with rotors turning
Height: 4.31 m
Empty weight: 4,656 kg
Max take-off weight: 6,690 kg
Max weapon load: 753 kg
Maximum speed: 315 km/h
Maximum rate of climb: 196 m per minute, vertical
Service ceiling: 4,500 m
Hovering ceiling in ground effect: 4,500 m
Hovering ceiling out of ground effect: 914 m with 8 missiles and rockets
Maximum range: 587 km

Opposite: A U.S. Marines SuperCobra.

Right: A trio of SuperCobras on manoeuvres.

Bell OH - 58D Kiowa Warrior　　　USA

In 1981, a US Army helicopter improvement (AHIP) contract was signed with Bell covering the upgrade of OH-58A Kiowa reconnaissance helicopters to **OH-58D** standard, for return to service from 1985. It was later decided that **OH-58Ds** should be armed for a wider hunter-killer role, becoming **Kiowa Warriors** and with modifications starting in 1987. Some 366 have so far been upgraded, but the final total could exceed 500.

Powered by a 485 kW Allison 250-C30R or X turboshaft engine and with a fast-folding four-blade main rotor featuring elastomeric bearings and all-composite blades, **OH-58D Kiowa Warrior's** principal system is a multi-sensor mast-mounted sight with thermal imaging, high-resolution TV and laser rangefinder/designator modes. The sight allows extended stand-off reconnaissance, surveillance, threat/target assessment and intelligence gathering by day or night, and in adverse weather conditions. The crew benefit also from cockpit multi-function screens for data and imagery display, while a high-accuracy navigation suite provides global positioning and target location.

Armament choices are substantial, encompassing four Hellfire anti-armour missiles, or four Stinger air-to-air missiles, or two 7-round rocket pods, or an 0.50 in machine-gun pod, or a mix of any two. Survivability in a hostile environment has been enhanced by the adoption of an infra-red jammer, pulse and CW radar warning receivers, laser warning detector and inherent infra-red suppression.

Fifteen **OH-58D Kiowa Warriors** known as "Prime Chance" were sent to the Persian Gulf where they operated from US Navy vessels to protect sea lanes and the ships as Task Force 118 during 1988-91. Elements of this force (redesignated 4/17) later undertook special operations during Operation Desert Storm, when 115 US Army **OH-58Ds** accumulated nearly 9,000 flying hours.

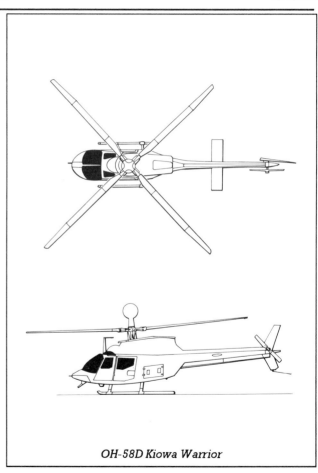

OH-58D Kiowa Warrior

Specification

Current users: US Army and Taiwan (newly constructed)
Crew: Two
Main rotor diameter: 10.67 m
Length: 12.85 m, with rotors turning
Height: 3.94 m
Empty weight: 1,492 kg
Max take-off weight: 2,495 kg
Maximum speed: 236 km/h
Maximum rate of climb: 488 m per minute at sea level
Service ceiling: 4,570 m
Hovering ceiling in ground effect: 3,050 m
Hovering ceiling out of ground effect: 2,100 m
Maximum range: 414 km

Kiowa Warrior firing from the port seven-round rocket pod.

Boeing Sikorsky RAH-66 Comanche USA

Although **Comanche** will not achieve early operational capability for evaluation until at least the year 2001, and then only by six pre-production helicopters for reconnaissance pending the full production decision in 2003, it is of such importance that no book of this type should omit it. The 1,292 **Comanches** required are intended to replace several of the US Army's main current helicopters, namely the attack AH-1 HueyCobra, observation OH-6 and the OH-58D Kiowa Warrior hunter-killer (see earlier pages). The first of two prototypes was rolled out on 25 May 1995.

    Comanche is a joint Boeing and Sikorsky programme, to provide a state-of-the-art all-weather multi-role battlefield helicopter, with low observability features and high performance. The primary mission is armed reconnaissance but air combat and light attack capabilities are also important. Power is provided by two 690 kW LHTEC T800 turboshafts, driving a 5-blade bearingless main rotor with composite blades and the 8-blade Fantail tail rotor system that is tolerant to strikes from 12.7 mm ammunition and can continue to function after the loss of a blade. The airframe itself is constructed of composites and is tolerant to hits of up to 23 mm.

    Heart of the helicopter is its advanced sensor systems, encompassing Westinghouse Longbow fire-control radar, focal-plane-array FLIR, low-light-level TV, laser rangefinder/designator, and aided target detection/classification, permitting day/night and adverse weather operations. The crew in tandem cockpits have liquid crystal multi-function displays, helmet-integrated displays and sighting systems, and modern sidestick cyclic pitch controllers. Highly accurate navigation and anti-jam communications systems assist mission success. A stowable gun turret will have a 20 mm multi-barrel cannon with 500 rounds of ammunition; air-to-air and attack armament will be carried internally. Two sizes of detachable stub wings, are available to permit a maximum total of 16 Stinger air-to-air missiles, or 14 Hellfire anti-armour missiles, or 62 rockets, or a combination thereof.

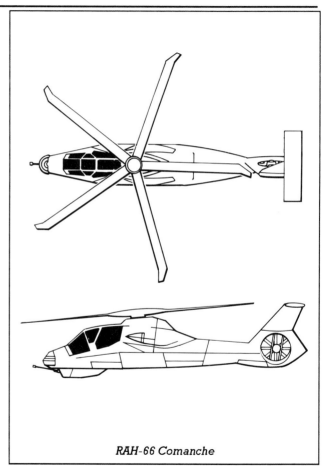

RAH-66 Comanche

Specification

First prototype: 1995
Current users: Intended for the US Army
Crew: Two
Main rotor diameter: 11.90 m
Length: 14.28 m
Height: 3.39 m
Empty weight: 3,402 kg
Max take-off weight: 4,587 kg for armed reconnaissance mission. Can be much higher for ferry flights
Maximum speed: 328 km/h
Maximum rate of climb: 360 m per minute vertical
Range: 2,334 km ferry for self-deployment

A prototype Boeing Sikorsky RAH-66 Comanche.

CASA C-101 Aviojet & ENAER Halcón   Spain/Chile

The C-101 was developed with assistance from MBB of Germany and Northrop of the USA to provide a combat-capable basic/advanced/lead-in jet trainer for the Spanish Air Force and export. The airframe became a modular design with an impressive 10,000 flying hour structural life, and the aircraft as a whole requires a low number of maintenance hours per flying hour in a bid to keep operating costs low. Typical tandem seating has been provided for the trainee and instructor, with the instructor in the elevated rear cockpit having overall command control.

The initial trainer version was the **C-101 EB** with a 15.57 kN thrust Garrett (now known as AlliedSignal) TFE731-2J turbofan engine, entering Spanish service from 1980. By uprating the engine to a 16.46 kN TFE731-3J, the Aviojet became a suitable armed trainer as the **C-101 BB**, chosen by Honduras and also put into local assembly in Chile as the **T-36 Halcón**. However, major combat capability arrived with the **C-101 CC**, with a 21.13 kN TFE731-5J engine, again assembled in Chile as the **A-36 Halcón** and also selected for service by Jordan. Possible roles include attack and tactical support with bombs, rocket launchers or two Maverick missiles on up to six underwing pylons, while for air defence two Sidewinder or Magic air-to-air missiles can be deployed. A stores bay under the fuselage can house detachable mission payloads, most commonly a 30 mm DEFA 553 cannon pod with 130 rounds of ammunition or twin 12.7 mm machine-guns in a pod with 220 rounds each, though it can also house a reconnaissance camera or laser designator. All weapons and/or mission equipment carried have to be within the total weight limit of 1,814 kg.

The latest version is the **C-101 DD**, basically the CC but with an integrated navigation/attack system based on a head-up display and with mission and air data computers, inertial platform and more, integrated using a MIL STD 1553B digital databus.

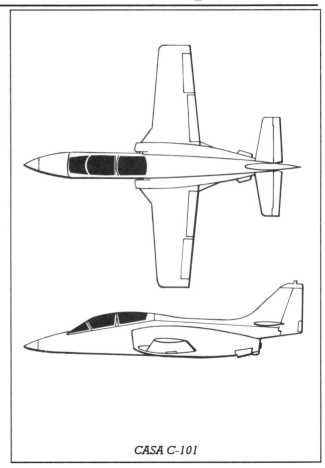

CASA C-101

Specification (C-101 CC)

First prototype: 27 June 1977 for prototype C-101, and 16 November 1983 for CC
Current users: See text
Crew: Two
Wing span: 10.6 m
Length: 12.5 m
Height: 4.25 m
Empty weight: 3,470 kg
Max take-off weight: 6,300 kg
Max weapon load: 1,814 kg
Maximum speed: 833 km/h
Maximum rate of climb: 1,950 m per minute
Service ceiling: 13,400 m
Maximum range: 3,700 km with optional drop tanks

C-101 BB operated by Honduras in full combat camouflage.

Chengdu J-7 and MiG-21   China/Russia

During the mid-1950s Mikoyan were testing experimental fighters to assess the relative benefits of swept wing and delta configurations. On 24 June 1956 the Soviet public at Tushino was given its first look at the E-5 development aircraft, destined to be the forerunner of the MiG-21 lightweight close air combat fighter which would replace the MiG-19.

The MiG-21 became Mikoyan's first production fighter to have delta wings, though still retaining a full tail unit that included an all-moving tailplane. But, most importantly, MiG-21 was intended from the outset to carry early model air-to-air guided missiles and have radar housed in the nose centrebody shock-cone to provide limited all-weather capability. Other requirements included a very high rate of climb from the single Tumansky R-11 engine and good manoeuvrability.

In the event, the MiG-21F izdelye 72 original production version manufactured during 1959-60, and known to NATO by the codename Fishbed-C, had to be fielded with only cannon armament and no radar, but subsequent MiG-21 versions introduced K-13 Atoll missiles and RP-21 radar, so bringing the fighter up to the required standard. And, such was the success of the MiG-21 that three Soviet factories went on to produce a total of 10,158 aircraft over many years and in many upgraded forms, while others were built in Czechoslovakia and India.

Some 3,500 MiG-21s remain in service with 33 air forces around the world (though none for combat with Russian forces), with close air support as a principal role, while upgrade programmes to maintain combat efficiency are offered by Russia, Israel, Bulgaria and others. The widely used MiG-21bis Fishbed-L has a 67.18 kN with afterburning Soyuz/Gavrilov R-25-300 turbojet engine, RP-22SM or SMA Sapfir-21 radar with a search range of up to 25 km, and up to 1,200 kg of armament on four underwing pylons that can include

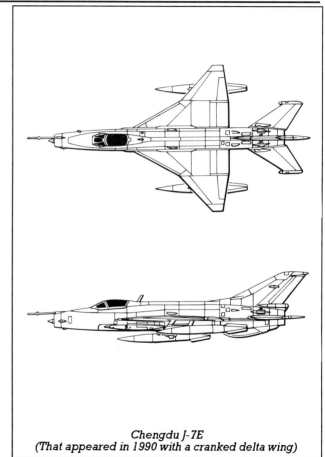

Chengdu J-7E
(That appeared in 1990 with a cranked delta wing)

R-60M Aphid, R-13M Atoll or other air-to-air missiles or alternatively a wide range of other weapons for attack missions, plus a 23 mm cannon under the fuselage.

On 17 January 1966 China flew the first example of its J-7, built at Shenyang and based on the MiG-21F-13 but incorporating much Chinese engineering work after the Soviet Union had halted assistance. In the following year production moved to Chengdu, where several new models followed until some 1,000 had been built for home use and export as J-7/F-7 types to Albania, Bangladesh, Egypt, Iran, Iraq, Myanmar, Pakistan, Sri Lanka, Tanzania and Zimbabwe. Probably the most capable version is the F-7P Airguard, operated by Pakistan and which has adopted Grifo radar and other western avionics plus four Sidewinder missiles. Of importance also is Chengdu's new FC-1, due to make its first flight in 1997 and expected to enter service with China and Pakistan in the next century. This is clearly a development of J-7/F-7/former Super-7 for air superiority, close air support and interdiction, with a Russian 80 kN thrust Klimov RD-93 turbofan engine and 3,500 kg weapon load.

Artist's impression of Chengdu FC-1s.

49

Specification
(MiG-21bis, where appropriate)

First prototype: 9 January 1956 for E-5 experimental model
Current users: Afghanistan, Algeria, Angola, Azerbaidjan, Bangladesh, Bulgaria, Cambodia, Congo, Croatia, Cuba, Czech Republic, Ethiopia, Guinea, Hungary, India, Laos, Libya, Madagascar, Mali, Mongolia, Montenegro, Mozambique, North Korea, Poland, Romania, Serbia, Slovak Republic, Somalia, Sudan, Syria, Vietnam, Yemen and Zambia for all versions of MiG-21
Crew: Pilot
Wing span: 7.154 m
Length: 15.75 m
Height: 4.103 m
Empty weight: 5,843 kg
Max take-off weight: 10,400 kg
Max weapon load: See text
Maximum speed: Mach 2.05
Maximum rate of climb: 13,500 m per minute at sea level
Service ceiling: 17,500 m
Maximum range: 1,470 km with two drop tanks

Above: *Israel Aircraft Industries MiG-21-2000 upgrade, with Elta EL/M-2032 radar, wrap-around windshield and new computer and cockpit displays.*

Opposite: *Chengdu F-7BS with ground attack bombs and rocket launchers plus underfuselage drop tank, used by Sri Lanka. (credit Denis Hughes)*

Eurocopter AS532 Variants

The Eurocopter **AS 532 Cougar** is the military version of the Super Puma, itself developed from the original SA 330 Puma of 1965 first appearance. A twin-turbine multi-role helicopter of medium size, it is available and operated in two main variants, as the **AS 532U2** for a mainly military utility role (28 troops, or 29 troops as the Mk 2) or for search/rescue, and as the **AS 532A2 Cougar Mk 2** for either naval anti-submarine/anti-ship missions or for assault, fire suppression and fire support roles armed with rocket launchers or gun/cannon pods. Interestingly, the utility model has also formed the basis of a battlefleld surveillance derivative, under the French Army's Horizon programme, operated by the Rapid Reaction Force.

The large number of Super Puma/Cougar users include the Turkish Army, whose ULs are being assembled locally. Power is provided by two Turbomeca Makila 1A2 turboshafts, each rated at 1,375 kW at take-off.

Although French production converted from Puma to Super Puma in the very early 1980s, Atlas of South Africa has developed a **Gunship** derivative initially based on the original Turbomeca Turmo IVC turboshaft-engined Puma, by developing a low-cost weapon suite that still allows the transport role to be retained. The **Puma Gunship** modification offers a nose-mounted sighting system for daylight operations, with the option of night vision equipment. The 20 mm cannon is mounted in a computer-controlled turret and aimed by a helmet sighting system or helicopter stabilized optronic sight, while two pylons on each of the fuselage-mounted weapon beams provide for the carriage of 68 mm rockets in four 18-round launchers (or other rockets) for area suppression, or eight ZT-3 or TOW missiles plus two rocket pods for an anti-armour role. Air-to-air missiles can also be beam-mounted for self defence.

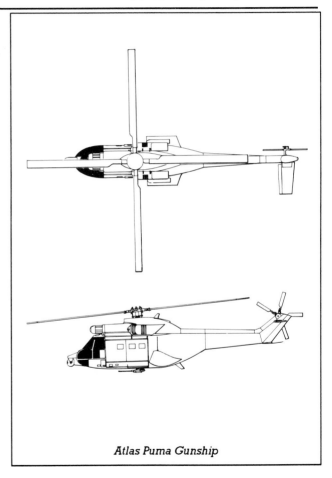

Atlas Puma Gunship

IAR of Romania is the only remaining production source of the original Turmo-engined Puma, built under licence.

The **IAR-330L Puma** can have navigation or surveillance radar, a 20 mm turreted cannon and a wide range of weapons that encompasses eight anti-armour missiles, four 70 mm, 57 mm or 122 mm rocket launchers, 7.62 mm gun pods, 100 kg bombs, or mines.

A new upgraded model is the **Puma 2000** with higher-rated engines, more modern cockpit controls and displays (including head-up), Hellfire anti-armour missiles as a weapon option, and optional forward-looking infra-red and TV sensors, and laser rangefinder/target designator.

Atlas Puma gunship.

Specification
(IAR-330L, as appropriate)

First prototype: 13 September 1978 for Super Puma
Current users: Some 43 countries operate civil and/or military Eurocopter Pumas/Super Pumas/Cougars. France, Pakistan, Romania, South Africa and Sudan operate IAR Pumas.
Crew: Normally two crew, plus 16-20 troops when required.
Main rotor diameter: 15.08 m
Length: 18.22 m, with rotors turning
Height: 5.14 m
Empty weight: 3,615 kg
Max take-off weight: 7,400 kg
Max weapon load: See text
Maximum cruise speed: 258 km/h
Maximum rate of climb: 366 m per minute
Service ceiling: 4,800 m
Hovering ceiling in ground effect: 2,300 m
Hovering ceiling out of ground effect: 1,700 m
Maximum range: 550 km

Opposite: Modular strap-on weapon system for Puma produced by Atlas of South Africa.

Right: Atlas Puma gunship strap-on weapon system.

Eurocopter AS 550 & AS 555 Fennec   International

AS 550 Fennec is the military version of the single-engined AS 350 Ecureuil light helicopter, fitted with taller undercarriage skids. This, and its twin-engined AS 555 Fennec companion, are operated by at least 23 countries, with users including the French Army that recently ordered six new **AS 550s** for anti-armour missions to strengthen its existing helicopter force.

Eurocopter offers five versions of **AS 550**, including the usually unarmed **AS 550 U2** for utility or observation, and the **AS 550 M2** and **AS 550 S2** naval models. The most important from the point of view of this book are, however, the **AS 550 A2** and **AS 550 C2**. A2 is a battlefield helicopter, powered by a 546 kW Turbomeca Arriel 1D1 turboshaft engine and with a 3-blade composites main rotor with Starflex bearingless rotor head. The crew can adopt night vision goggles for operations in darkness. Typical armament is a 20 mm gun pod and rocket launcher, with which it can patrol for over two hours at a distance of 50 km from base. The ability to carry five troops or military cargo is retained. The **AS 550 C2** is far more potent, though again able to carry troops or cargo when required and is powered by the same Arriel 1D1 engine. It can be used in an air-to-air role but is most prominent as a light anti-tank helicopter, installed with a HeliTOW sighting system above the cockpit and four TOW missiles on fuselage outriggers. In this weapon configuration, it has an endurance of two and a half hours while holding twenty minutes reserve fuel.

AS 555 Fennec is a twin-engined version of AS 550, using two Arrius 1A1 turboshaft engines, each with a 357 kW rating at take-off.

The battlefield model is the **AS 555 AN** which can patrol for one and a half hours at 50 km range from base, while the anti-tank or air-to-air model is the **AS 555 CN**. Unarmed utility and armed/unarmed naval versions are also offered.

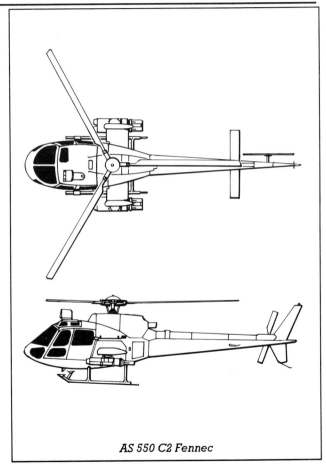

AS 550 C2 Fennec

Specification
(AS 550)

First prototype: 27 June 1974 for the AS 350
Current users: See text
Crew: Two
Main rotor diameter: 10.69 m
Length: 12.94 m, with rotors turning
Height: 3.34 m
Empty weight: 1,220 kg
Max take-off weight: 2,500 kg
Max weapon load: See text
Maximum cruise speed: 246 km/h
Maximum rate of climb: 510 m per minute
Service ceiling: 4,600 m
Hovering ceiling in ground effect: 3,000 m
Hovering ceiling out of ground effect: 2,300 m
Maximum range: See text

AS 550 C2 Fennec shown fitted with the Anti-tank configuration and Helitow system.

Eurocopter AS 565 Panther International

Panther is the military version of the 10-13 seat AS 365 N2 Dauphin 2 civil multi-purpose helicopter, with higher rated engines and more composite material in its construction. Because of its use in potentially hostile environments, survivability features abound, ranging from the paint finish and engine detail to suppress infra-red, radar and noise signatures, through to armour protection and crashworthy airframe, seats and fuel system. In addition to these are the usual infra-red jammer, radar warning receiver and chaff/flare dispenser.

Panther is much larger and heavier than the Fennecs previously detailed, with a retractable undercarriage, four-blade main rotor with Starflex hub, and an eleven-blade fan-in-fin anti-torque system known as Fenestron. The horizontal stabiliser has endplates that are off-centred.

The battlefield model is designated **AS 565 AA** and, like all **AS 565 Panthers**, is powered by two 558 kW Turbomeca Arriel 1M1 or 633 kW Arriel 2C turboshaft engines. It can carry an impressive air-to-air armament of eight Mistral missiles, though more usual would be 20 mm cannon pods and rocket launchers.

AS 565 CA is the anti-tank version with an above-cockpit sighting system and HOT missiles, while the unarmed military model for utility and observation is the **AS 565 UA**. As with Fennec, armed and unarmed naval models of Panther are available as the SA and MA respectively, plus a dedicated search and rescue model known as AS 565 SB.

A further development is the **Panther 800**, with 995 kW LHTEC T800-LHT-800 engines, as had been proposed to meet a US Army requirement in co-operation with the former Vought company.

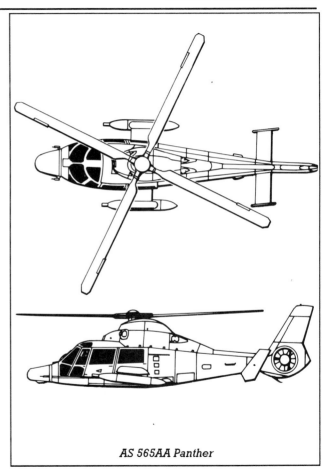

AS 565AA Panther

Specification

First prototype: 29 February 1984
Current users: Include the Brazilian Army with AS 565 AAs, and Saudi Arabia, France, and the United Arab Emirates for armed naval types
Crew: Two
Main rotor diameter: 11.94 m
Length: 13.68 m, with rotors turning
Height: 3.97 m
Empty weight: 2,255 kg
Max take-off weight: 4,250 kg

Max weapon load: See text
Maximum cruise speed: 279 km/h at sea level
Maximum rate of climb: 420 m per minute
Service ceiling: perhaps 3,700 m
Hovering ceiling in ground effect: 2,600 m
Hovering ceiling out of ground effect: 1,850 m
Maximum range: 875 km

A utility version of the AS 565 UA Panther used for light tactical transport and casualty-carrying missions.

Eurocopter SA 341 & SA 342 Gazelle International

First flown on 7 April 1967, the **Gazelle** was the product of an Anglo-French co-operative programme between Westland and Aérospatiale. This co-operation produced a five seat light military utility, communications and training helicopter in the original SA 341 form, with armed options. However, Aérospatiale retained design and production leadership. SA 341s are still in major use with the British forces and French Army, the latter's 480 kW Turbomeca Astazou III-engined SA 341F2s having the option of a Giat 20 mm gun. Those operated abroad include SA 341H Partizans built under licence in the former Yugoslavia by Soko from the early 1970s, designated HO-42s when fitted with weapons for attack and armed reconnaissance roles.

In 1973 Kuwait received a military version of **Gazelle** designated SA 342K, featuring a 650 kW Astazou XIVH engine. SA 342 became the main production model and is the only type still offered and built. SA 342M is a current French Army version for daylight anti-armour use with HOT missiles and a gyrostabilised sight, having joined operational units from 1980, although about 70 of over 150 on strength are now receiving Viviane roof sights with direct path, infra-red channel and laser rangefinder to allow HOT firing at night. New rotor blades are also being retrofitted. A further 30 French helicopters have each been armed with four Mistral air-to-air missiles for this change of role.

SA 342L2 is the current export model, also powered by a 640 kW Turbomeca Astazou XIV M turboshaft, and offered with night vision goggles. The earlier SA 342L1 was built in the former Yugoslavia in GAMA anti-tank form with four AT-3 Sagger-type missiles or two 57 mm rocket launchers, plus optionally two Strela air-to-air missiles, all mounted on movable outriggers. Another Soko version was the HERA for reconnaissance, while trainers completed the line-up.

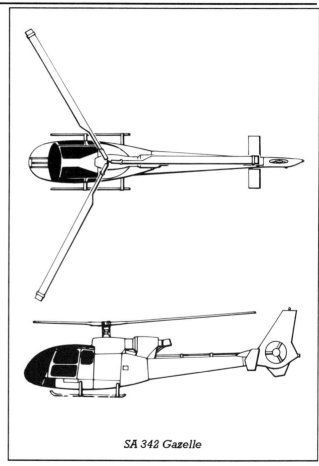

SA 342 Gazelle

Specification
(SA 342M)

First prototype: See text
Current users: Some 25 countries operate military Gazelles
Crew: Pilot and co-pilot/weapon aimer
Main rotor diameter: 10.48 m
Length: 11.91 m, with rotors turning
Height: 3.19 m
Empty weight: 1,009 kg
Max take-off weight: 2,100 kg
Max weapon load: See text

Maximum cruise speed: 245 km/h at sea level
Maximum rate of climb: 462 m per minute at sea level
Service ceiling: 4,450 m
Hovering ceiling in ground effect: 3,150 m
Hovering ceiling out of ground effect: 2,370 m
Maximum range: 670 km

A French Army Gazelle armed for anti-tank warfare.

Eurocopter BO 105 PAH-1   Germany

This former German MBB helicopter, now incorporated into the Eurocopter line-up, is a light five/six-seater that has been built in very large numbers for both civil and military operators around the world, including many for law enforcement. Special features include clamshell loading doors in the rear of the cabin pod, and a four-blade hingless rigid main rotor that can be folded. Equipment options include FLIR, for night operations and weapons when appropriate.

The latest version is the EC Super Five, developed to replace the **BO 105 CBS**, with improved main rotor blades that offer increased thrust and reduced vibration and fuel consumption. Each version is powered by two 313 kW Allison 250-C20B turboshaft engines.

Several countries fly armed **BO 105**s, including Sweden, where the Army received 20 **BO 105 CB**s during 1987-88 for anti-tank duties, each carrying the HeliTOW missile system (8 TOW missiles can be carried) plus Helios sight to provide night vision and laser capability. The Spanish Army also took **BO 105**s, including 14 for observation, 18 for armed reconnaissance and 28 **BO 105ATH**s for anti-tank missions. The **BO 105ATH**s have been receiving new blades, cockpit updates to allow the use of night vision goggles, global positioning navigation, radar and infra-red warning receivers or chaff/flare dispensers, and HOT missiles on lightweight launchers to enhance their capability.

The largest armed force, however, comprises German Army **BO 105 VBH**s for liaison and observation and PAH-1s for anti-armour operations. No fewer than 212 PAH-1s were delivered during 1980-84, first going to Heeresfliegerregiment 16. Crewed by the pilot and weapon operator, PAH-1s adopted stabilised sights mounted on the roof, suited to daylight operations, and HOT missiles (6 each). However, these helicopters have recently received new rotor blades plus other changes, with take-off weight increased from 2,400 kg to 2,500 kg. A large number now have HOT 2 missiles on revised launchers, but the expected retrofit of new roof-mounted sights for night firing did not take place.

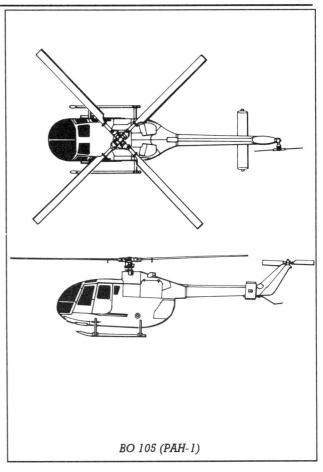

BO 105 (PAH-1)

Specification
(based on PAH-1)

First prototype: 16 February 1967
Current users: See text
Crew: See text
Main rotor diameter: 9.84 m
Length: 11.86 m, with rotors turning
Height: 3 m
Empty weight: 1,913 kg
Max take-off weight: 2,500 kg for PAH-1
Max weapon load: See text
Maximum cruise speed: 220 km/h
Maximum rate of climb: 540 m per minute
Service ceiling: 4,200 m
Hovering ceiling out of ground effect: 1,580 m
Maximum range: 555 km for CBS

The German Army's first generation anti-tank helicopter showing the HOT-2 digital weapons system and new rotor blades.

Eurocopter Tigre

Tigre is a new purpose-designed tandem two-seat combat helicopter in two distinct principal models, namely HAP for close support and helicopter escort and HAC for anti-armour. Development has been funded by the French and German governments. Development began in June 1995 together with a Memorandum of Understanding for the Trigat weapon system, allowing production deliveries from 1999. The French Army has a stated need for 140 HACs and 75 HAPs, while the German Army wants 212 helicopters as anti-armour PAH-2s or combined anti-armour/combat support UHUs. **Tigre** can operate in nuclear/ biological/chemical contaminated conditions.

Tigre is powered by two 872 kW MTU/Turbomeca/Rolls-Royce MTR 390 turboshaft engines, with an infra-red suppressor system using cold air to dilute the exhaust gas, which is then diverted upwards. Armour plate is installed between the engines. The main rotor is of four-blade hingeless, rigid, soft-in-plane type, with composite ballistic-tolerant blades. Eighty percent of the airframe is constructed of composite materials, with the lower area of the fuselage structure crash-dedicated to ensure that the crew survives impacts of 34 ft (10.5 m) per second vertical and 39 ft (12 m) per second longitudinal.

Advanced avionics systems include the use of colour multi-function displays and a helmet sight/display for each crew member. HAC uses the Osiris mast-mounted sight with infra-red, TV and laser rangefinder modes plus a nose-mounted FLIR sensor. HAP has a roof sight with infra-red camera and TV, direct optical mode, and laser rangefinder, and can also have a head-up sight/display.

Only HAP can deploy a turreted 30 mm gun, other armament carried on the four stub-wing pylons comprises a mix of 4 Mistral AAMs and rockets (44 rockets with Mistrals, or 68 without) for its roles of protecting anti-armour helicopters against attack from hostile helicopters and vehicles plus combat support. HAC can carry eight HOT or Trigat anti-armour missiles plus 4 Mistrals or Stingers, or a mix of Trigats and HOTs plus Mistrals or Stingers and a 20 mm gun pod.

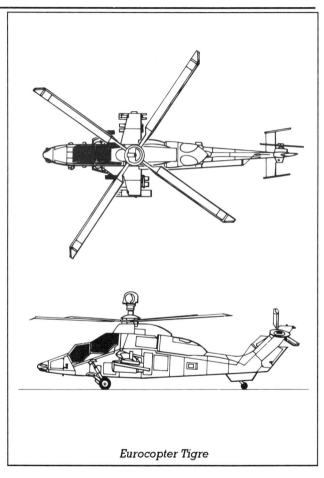

Eurocopter Tigre

Specification

First prototype: 27 April 1991
Current users: See text
Crew: Two
Main rotor diameter: 13 m
Length: 14 m, fuselage only
Height: 3.81 m
Empty weight: 3,300 kg
Max take-off weight: 6,000 kg
Max weapon load: See text
Maximum speed: 322 km/h design limit for HAP
Maximum rate of climb: 690 m per minute for HAP
Hovering ceiling out of ground effect: 3,500 m) for HAP
Maximum range: 800 km, without drop tanks

HAC with Trigat, Mistral and gun pod armament (credit Alain Ernoult).

Fairchild A-10A Thunderbolt II　　USA

A-10A was developed as a very heavily armed, high subsonic close air support aircraft of completely new type, with a devastating GAU-8/A Avenger seven-barrel cannon installed in the nose, depressed by two degrees for attacking ground targets (including tanks) and with 1,174 rounds of 30 mm armour-piercing ammunition. An additional 7,257 kg of weapons can be carried under eight wing pylons plus any of three underfuselage pylons, although not all fuselage pylons can be used simultaneously. Armament choices include six Maverick missiles, various types of conventional and guided bombs, Combined Munition Dispensers, and four Sidewinder air-to-air missiles. However, maximum weapon load is reduced to 5,482 kg when full fuel is required to achieve a long mission range or to maximise loiter period in a battle area.

Power comes from two 40.32 kN General Electric TF34-GE-100 turbofan engines, each housed in a pod that is mounted high on the rear fuselage, ahead of the twin fin tail unit. The unusual position was chosen to prevent engine damage while operating from semi-prepared airfields and also to make use of the wings and tailplane in masking the engines from infra-red homing missiles. Often flying at very low level, armour protects the flight control system, while the pilot has a titanium armoured cockpit able to withstand strikes from up to 23 mm gunfire. An electronic countermeasures jammer and chaff/flare offer further protection in a hostile environment.

A total of 713 **A-10As** was built for the USAF between 1975 and 1984, with large numbers being assigned subsequently to forward air control duties as **OA-10As**. These are identical to **A-10As** except that equipment includes ECM as well as Sidewinders for self-defence, and no other armament is carried although rockets are used to mark targets for other aircraft to attack. The active USAF can call upon some 131 **A-10As** and 101 **OA-10As**, while the Air National Guard flies 105 **A-10As** and the Air Force Reserve has 44 **A-10A/OA-10As**.

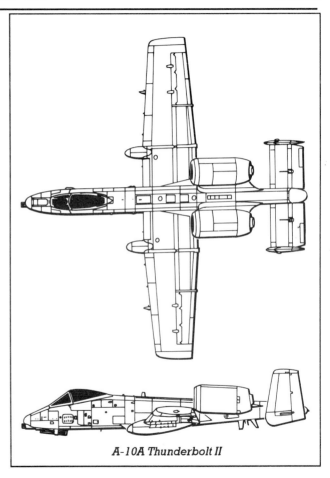

A-10A Thunderbolt II

Specification

First prototype: 10 May 1972
Current users: USA
Crew: Pilot
Wing span: 17.53 m
Length: 16.26 m
Height: 4.47 m
Empty weight: 12,700 kg
Max take-off weight: 23,586 kg
Max weapon load: See text
Maximum speed: 707 km/h
Maximum rate of climb: 1,830 m per minute
Maximum range: 763 km radius of action

Right: A duo of tank-busting A-10A Thunderbolt IIs.

FMA Pucará   Argentina

Pucará was the product of the former Fábrica Militar de Aviones SA (FMA), Argentina's government-owned and Air Force controlled aircraft manufacturing organization, before privatisation led to a new management structure under a contract with the US Lockheed company in December 1994. **Pucará** was designed as a simple and inexpensive counter-insurgency, close air support and reconnaissance aircraft, with two fuel-efficient turboprop engines and two crew members seated in tandem to share the workload. Important innovations were its ability to use unprepared airstrips, provision for JATO boosters to allow take-off after a mere 80 metre run, and armour protection on the cockpit floor to protect the crew from 7.62 mm enemy fire.

Delivery of 108 **Pucarás** to the Argentine Air Force took place over ten years from 1976, including 48 ordered after the Falklands/Malvinas conflict to make good losses and increase the number available to the Air Force, since when surplus aircraft have been exported in tiny numbers to Colombia, Sri Lanka and Uruguay. Each **Pucará** has fixed armament of four 7.62 mm machine-guns and two 20 mm cannon in the nose, while up to a 1,500 kg total weapon load can be carried on two underwing and one underfuselage pylons, with armament choices including Pescador or other air-to-surface missiles, torpedoes for an anti-shipping role, rocket launchers, various types of bombs, or gun pods. A reflector sight was part of the original specification.

Typically, a drop tank is carried under the fuselage to increase range, although all three pylons can carry tanks for ferrying, whilst operating with just the pilot on board also helps increase the range/payload possibilities. A specialised single-seat derivative and a more powerful two-seater were also developed but not adopted for squadron use, leaving the two-seat IA 58A with 720 kW Turbomeca Astazou XVIG turboprop engines as the only service model (about 40 used by the Argentine Air Force in 1995).

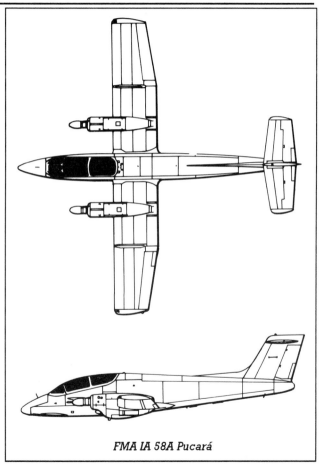

FMA IA 58A Pucará

Specification

First prototype: 20 August 1969.
Current users: See text
Crew: Two
Wing span: 14.5 m
Length: 14.25 m
Height: 5.36 m
Empty weight: 4,020 kg
Max take-off weight: 6,800 kg

Max weapon load: See text
Maximum speed: 500 km/h
Maximum rate of climb: 1,075 m per minute
Service ceiling: above 9,750 m
Maximum range: up to 972 km with 1,730 litres of fuel

Argentine Pucará, using multi-store ejectors to increase the number of fuselage and wing weapons.

IAI Kfir   Israel

The **Kfir** resulted from the last of a series of important programmes based around the French Mirage design, subsequently aimed at providing the Israeli Air Force with combat aircraft of domestic manufacture. The need for self reliance stemmed from an embargo placed on the dispatch to Israel of a new batch of French Dassault Mirage 5s at a time of political turbulence in the region. The first step by Israel towards autonomy had been to construct spares for Mirages already serving with the Air Force, followed by the local manufacture of complete Mirage-type airframes installed with SNECMA Atar turbojet engines but incorporating Israeli avionics, systems and equipment, resulting in a combat aircraft known as Nesher. Many ex-Israeli Neshers were sold to Argentina as Daggers from 1978 and upgraded.

Nesher had entered Israeli Air Force service from 1972, by which time a Mirage III had been under test for two years with a General Electric J79 turbojet installed in place of the normal Atar. Use of the differently dimensioned J79 had forced significant modifications to the airframe, but the resulting marriage between airframe and engine proved very satisfactory. The next logical step was, therefore, to install a J79 into a Nesher airframe, the resulting prototype first flying in mid-1973 as the prototype **Kfir**. A production **Kfir** was displayed two years later, seen to have a shorter but wider rear fuselage than the Mirage 5 and many other modifications.

The first **Kfir** version, the C1, equipped just two squadrons, and many were later upgraded to the next C2 standard, which introduced canards, dogtooth wings and other changes. Some C2s remain in store in Israel and some others were exported to Ecuador, but most were upgraded to C7 form using the more powerful J79-J1E engine of 83.41 kN with afterburning, plus upgrades to the avionics and cockpit. C7s will remain standard equipment of the Israeli Air Force

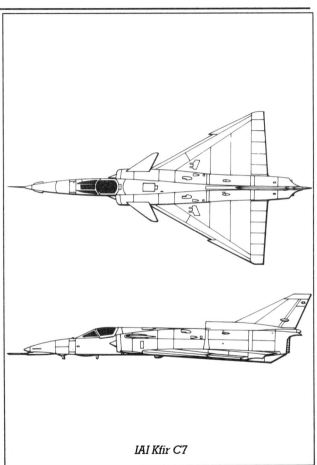

IAI Kfir C7

in a dual attack/interceptor role until at least the year 2000.

The C7 boasts nine weapon pylons suited to a 6,085 kg load and with a wide range of weapon choices which includes Griffin and Guillotine laser guided bombs, Pyramid TV-guided bombs, Maverick or Shrike or similar air-to-ground missiles, rockets, two or four Python 3 or Shafrir 2 missiles or other air-to-air missiles.

Fixed armament comprises two 30 mm DEFA 552 cannon, while the Elta EL/M-2021 radar is of pulse-Doppler fire control type.

Colombia also deploys **Kfir** C7s, and all users have numbers of corresponding TC two-seaters for training.

The latest Kfir upgrades being offered are the C10 and **Kfir** 2000, with improved EL/M-2032 multi-mode, track-while-scan radar, new fire control and stores management computer, new head-up and head-down displays and much more besides, though neither version had entered service at the time of writing.

Exports would comprise upgraded surplus Israeli Air Force **Kfirs**.

Battle-ready Israeli Kfir.

Opposite: A "tooled-up" Kfir hunting near the Golan Heights.

Below: Latest version of Kfir multi-mission fighter.

Specification

First prototype: 1973
Current users: See text
Crew: Pilot
Wing span: 8.22 m
Length: 15.65 m
Height: 4.55 m
Max take-off weight: 16,500 kg
Max weapon load: See text
Maximum speed: over Mach 2.3
Maximum rate of climb: 14,000 m per minute

Service ceiling: 17,700 m
Maximum range: typically 1,186 km radius of action for attack

JAS 39 Gripen   Sweden

Gripen is the latest Swedish multi-role combat aircraft, and the first in the world to combine attack, interception and reconnaissance as principal roles in a single aircraft. This requires the same pilot to perform any of these roles as ordered, using push-button control to program the computer to select the mission characteristics. To permit this, **Gripen** has completely integrated avionics, via three MIL STD 1553 databuses, the Ericsson suite comprising the SDS 80 computing system, PS-05/A pulse-Doppler radar, electronic displays and more besides. The three colour head-down displays have selectable and interchangeable presentations that can be reconfigured in flight, while the wide-angle head-up display presents flight and weapon-aiming symbology. During attack missions, data on ground targets obtained by the radar can be tranferred via a data link to other **Gripens**, thereby allowing the others to operate in a radar-silent mode to enhance surprise.

Thirty percent of **Gripen's** airframe is constructed of composite materials, including the clipped delta wings and close-coupled all-moving canards. The large number of control surfaces are fly-by-wire activated.

Six of the weapon stations are wing-mounted, comprising four underwing pylons plus two wingtip launch rails for Rb 74 Sidewinder air-to-air missiles. Two pylons under the air intakes usually carry avionics pods, while a further pylon occupies a position under the fuselage.

Attack weapons can include Rb 75 Maverick air-to-surface missiles or other types (including RBS-15F for anti-shipping), cluster weapon dispensers, various types of bombs, and rocket launchers. In an interceptor role, AMRAAMs are among the choices.

Power for **Gripen** comes from a single Volvo RM12, based on the General Electric F404 turbofan. This has an afterburning thrust rating of 80.54 kN. The aircraft can be refuelled, re-armed and readied for a repeat mission by a technician and five conscripts in just ten

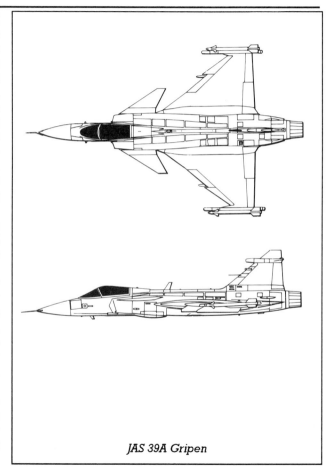

JAS 39A Gripen

minutes, while in an emergency it can operate from an 800 m length of main road, thereby reducing the need to build large numbers of costly and vulnerable dispersal runways in case of attack.

Production deliveries began in June 1993, and conversion of Swedish pilots from Viggens to **Gripens** started in 1995. The first unit, F7, will gain operational capability in 1997.

Delivery of production JAS 39B tandem two-seat trainer derivatives will start in 1998.

The Swedish Air Force requires up to 300 **Gripens** for 16 squadrons, with the first 140 for delivery by the year 2002. Thereafter, the single-seaters will be to JAS 39C standard.

The first export customer is likely to be Hungary.

Opposite: *JAS 39 Gripen for operational capability from 1997.*

Right: *JAS 39 Gripen aircraft undergoing advanced tests during 1995.*

Opposite: A fully armed Gripen of the Swedish Air Force.

Specification

First prototype: 9 December 1988
Current users: See text
Crew: Pilot in JAS 39A
Wing span: 8.40 m
Length: 14.1 m
Height: 4.5 m
Empty weight: 6,620 kg
Max take-off weight: 12,500 kg
Max weapon load: See text
Maximum speed: Supersonic

Below: A flight of Gripens on the runway.

Kamov Ka-29 and Ka-32A7   Russia

One of the shortcomings of the Ka-25 ship-borne helicopter was that it was not particularly suited to adaptation for amphibious assault , though it performed well in primary anti-submarine and other roles. **Ka-29**, as a variant of the much improved Ka-27 (and known to NATO under the codename Helix-B), addressed this shortcoming and has been deployed as a naval armed assault and transport helicopter. It can carry up to 16 troops or 2,000 kg of internal freight (or weapons) from a ship to land during amphibious operations, and can offer sufficient firepower to suppress enemy defences and undertake close air support.

Heart of the Ka-29 is the Shturm-V anti-armour system, used in conjunction with eight 9M114 Kokon (AT-6 Spiral) missiles carried in two four-tube clusters. A laser rangefinder is among optional equipment. Other armament that can be attached to the four pylons include up to four B-8 launchers (each with twenty 80 mm rockets), 30 mm cannon, 23 mm gun packs, bombs and incendiary weapons, while a trainable 7.62 mm four-barrel Gatling-type gun with 1,800 rounds of ammuniton is mounted in the nose behind a small door. For protection in a hostile environment, an infra-red jammer has been provided, and the cockpit and engine areas are armoured against hits from ground fire.

It is believed that about 30 Ka-29s are operational, all with the Russian Navy, having begun deployment in 1985 with both the Northern and Pacific fleets. As with other Kamov helicopters, Ka-29 has two contra-rotating rotors and thereby requires no separate anti-torque tail rotor. Power is provided by two Klimov/Izotov TV3-117VK turboshaft engines, each maximum rated at 1,659 kW.

A basically civil version of the Ka-27 became the Ka-32 (Helix-C), first flown on 11 January 1980. Its many uses include maritime patrol, though it is more readily associated with transport, flying-crane, offshore, rescue and firefighting. However, a surprising variant was recently revealed as the armed **Ka-32A7** with search radar under the nose. Clearly suited to anti-shipping, its optional gun pods and rocket launchers signifies adaptation also to armed support.

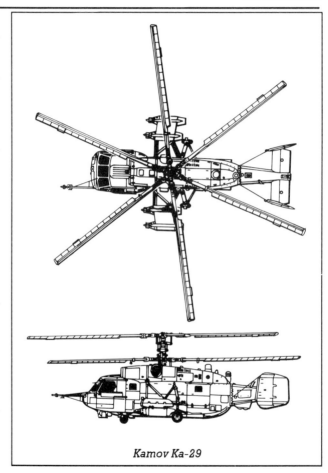

Kamov Ka-29

Specification
(Ka-29)

First prototype: 1976
Current users: Russia
Crew: Pilot and weapon system operator
Rotor diameter: 15.90 m each
Length: 12.25 m, rotors folded
Height: 5.44 m
Max take-off weight: 12,600 kg
Max weapon load: See text
Maximum speed: 280 km/h
Maximum rate of climb: 930 m per minute at sea level
Service ceiling: 4,300 m
Hovering ceiling out of ground effect: 3,700 m
Maximum range: 460 km, typical

Ka-32A7 with missile, rocket and gun options. (Credit Piotr Butowski).

Kamov Ka-50 and Ka-52 Werewolf   Russia

Although Russian state acceptance trials had been completed by 1993, the **Ka-50** single-seat anti-armour and close air support helicopter was not expected to gain initial operational capability until 1996, as military budget cutbacks had earlier brought production to a temporary halt after only a small number of **Ka-50s** had been completed. Further production is being divided between the single-seat **Ka-50** and side-by-side two-seat **Ka-52**, although with a greater percentage of single-seaters.

Ka-50 is the world's first single-seat combat helicopter, the pilot having use of a Zvezda ejection seat once the rotor blades have been blown clear by explosive charge. Power comes from two 1,640 kW Klimov TV3-117VK turboshaft engines, the nozzles fitted with infra-red suppression cool air mixers. The helicopter retains Kamov's traditional twin contra-rotating rotor system, here incorporating composite blades with swept tips. A large amount of armour has been installed to protect the engines, cockpit, and other vital areas from 20 mm fire. Other survivability systems include chaff/flare dispensers at the wingtips.

An important feature of the **Ka-50** is its ability to move with the troops and operate away from base for up to two weeks at a time. Its avionics are based around multiple Orbita digital computers, while a data link with reconnaissance helicopters allows target information to be presented on the map and head-up displays. Fixed armament comprises a Shipunov 30 mm cannon, which uses similar ammunition to armoured personnel carriers.

Other weapons are carried on the four underwing pylons, with typical loads including twelve 9A4172 Vikhr-M (AT-12) laser-guided anti-tank missiles in two batches on the inner pylons and two 68 mm B-8 rocket launchers on the outer pylons, although other armament choices also encompass Kh-25ML (AS-10 Karen) laser-guided and

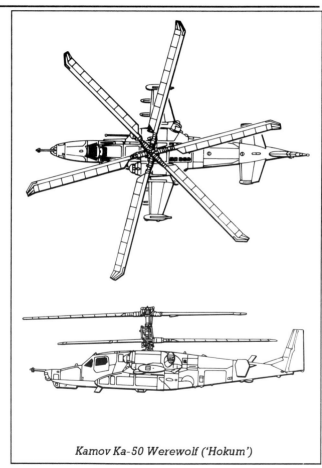

Kamov Ka-50 Werewolf ('Hokum')

Kh-25MP (AS-12 Kegler) anti-radar missiles, gun packs and more.

In an air-to-air role or for self-defence, R-73 (AA-11 Archer) and Igla V missiles can be deployed. The all important Shkval 3 electro-optical fire control unit has a TV channel, laser rangefinder/target designator, and laser beam riding system associated with the Vikhr missiles.

The pilot's helmet sight is integrated with Shkval, while night operations are possible with the adoption of a forward-looking infra-red sensor.

The two-seat **Ka-52** is being produced in two versions, one as a combat trainer and the other as a combat reconnaissance aircraft with reduced armament and armour but uprated engines.

Kamov Ka-52 mock-up displayed in 1995. (Piotr Butowski).

Specification (Ka-50)

First prototype: 17 June 1982
Current users: Russian Army
Crew: Pilot (two in Ka-52)
Rotor diameter: 14.43 m, each
Length: 15.96 m, rotors turning
Height: 4.93 m
Max take-off weight: 10,800 kg
Max weapon load: See text
Maximum speed: 310 km/h
Maximum rate of climb: 600 m per minute
Hovering ceiling out of ground effect: 4,000 m
Maximum range: 450 km, typical

Above: *Kamov Ka-50 in flight. (Piotr Butowski).*

Opposite: *An intimidating aspect of the Kamov Ka-50. (Piotr Butowski)*

Lockheed Martin F-16 Fighting Falcon   USA

More than 3,500 F-16s have been delivered since 1979, operated by the active US Air Force, Air National Guard and Air Force Reserve plus seventeen countries outside the USA. It was conceived to be a competitor in the Lightweight Fighter programme of the early 1970s, intended originally as a low-cost day fighter. Subsequent expansion of roles and equipment meant that the production version was far removed from the initial concept, having an AN/APG-66 radar for all-weather operations which by then also included ground attack.

The analogue fly-by-wire flight control system, introduced for the **F-16A** first production version and its **F-16B** two-seat training counterpart, enabled the designers to use a relaxed stability airframe design to improve manoeuvrability. The fly-by-wire system was upgraded to digital operation on the **F-16C**, which also introduced the AN/APG-68 radar and other enhancements to improve day and night attack capability, plus beyond-visual-range engagement.

F-16C CAS and **F-16D CAS** are the designations applied to hundreds of older USAF single-seat **F-16C**s and two-seat **F-16D**s modified specifically for close air support and battlefield interdiction. They are intended to replace A-10As and F-111E/Fs and feature Pave Penny laser spot tracker, LANTIRN and night vision goggles for night operations, data link improvements, new self-protection systems and much more besides.

The current production **F-16C** is powered by either a General Electric F110-GE-129 or Pratt & Whitney F100-PW-229 turbofan, of 128.93 kN or 129.45 kN thrust with afterburning respectively. Up to a 5,443 kg weapon load can be carried on nine stations, although two are wingtip launch rails for air-to-air missiles. Fighter and interceptor armament will be detailed in a separate book.

Attack weapons can be free-fall or precision guided bombs that include the new GBU-30, Maverick air-to-surface or various anti-radiation

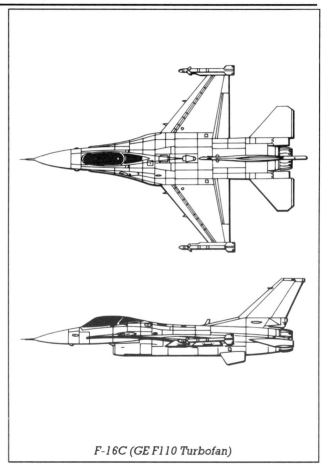

F-16C (GE F110 Turbofan)

(Skrike and HARM) or anti-ship (Harpoon or Penguin) missiles, munition dispensers and other types, with the future prospect of JSOW (AGM-154A Joint Standoff Weapon) with unitary or submunition warhead. Popeye is a further weapon choice, likely to be used by South Korea.

F-16ES is a new Enhanced Strategic version with extra fuel in conformal fuel tanks built above the wing/fuselage blend for reduced drag, featuring also a forward-looking infra-red sensor on the nose.

An F-16 Fighting Falcon of the Royal Norwegian Air Force patrolling in home territory.

Specification
(F-16C where appropriate)

First prototype: 20 January 1974
Current users: Bahrain, Belgium, Denmark, Egypt, Greece, Indonesia, Israel, South Korea, Netherlands, Norway, Pakistan, Portugal, Singapore, Taiwan, Thailand, Turkey, USA and Venezuela.
Crew: Pilot, or two in F-16B and D
Wing span: 10 m over wingtip missiles
Length: 15.02 m
Height: 5.09 m
Empty weight: 8,437 kg
Max take-off weight: 19,187 kg
Max weapon load: See text
Maximum speed: over Mach 2
Service ceiling: above 15,240 m
Maximum range: 3,218 km with maximum internal and external fuel for ferrying

Above: F-16 showing its impressive array of weapons stores.

Opposite: *F-16ES featuring conformal tanks, FLIR, with tip AAMs and underwing precision-guided bombs and drop tanks.*

Lockheed Martin F-117A Nighthawk

USA

The most unusual combat aircraft in service today, the **F-117A** is a subsonic night attack fighter intended to be deployed against priority targets. It was conceived to operate without detection under dense threat conditions, made possible through the world's first full use of stealth (low observable) technologies.

F-117 was developed from 1976 under a cloak of secrecy at Lockheed's Skunk Works, where two XST small-scale demonstrators were first built (the first flew in December 1977) to prove the feasibility of the general concept. Despite the highly radical nature of the **F-117** design, the computers and flight control, navigation and other systems came from F-16, F/A-18, B-52 and other existing aircraft to reduce development time and risk, while two non-afterburning General Electric F404-GE-F1D2 turbofan engines were selected to power the aircraft, each rated at 48.04 kN.

The problem of visual, radar, infra-red, acoustic, electromagnetic, smoke and contrail signatures had to be overcome if the aircraft was to remain undetected. The principal danger from the radar viewpoint was detection by high-altitude AWACS aircraft, with one solution found in adopting a unique faceted airframe comprising a large number of flat-plate panels set at sharp angles to each other to reflect radar beams away from the source, while further methods included special skin coatings. As the **F-117A** could not be allowed to deploy its own radar for fear of giving away its position, it uses forward-looking and downward-looking infra-red sensors with boresight laser designators and autotrackers to achieve target acquisition and designation. Low noise levels were made possible partly by having no engine afterburning, which also assisted infra-red signature reduction.

Other means of defeating IR came with the use of engine exhaust cooling and masked engine nozzles, overwing air intakes and other

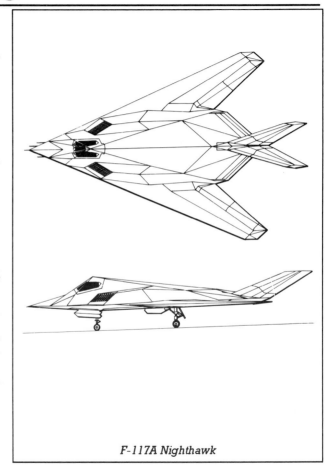

F-117A Nighthawk

features, the nozzles themselves being of very wide but shallow "slot" type to produce a thin exhaust plume that dispersed quickly to avoid contrails.

F-117A carries no guns or external weapons. Instead, the 2,268 kg weapon load is housed in the underfuselage bay and can include laser-guided bombs of up to 907 kg weight each, Maverick, HARM or other missiles, munition dispensers or nuclear bombs, with the possibility of Sidewinder air-to-air missiles for self defence.

Sixty F-117As were built, with 59 joining the USAF from 1982, although no F-117A was seen in public until 1990. By then the F-117A had undertaken its first combat missions, when two released laser-guided bombs on a barrack area in Panama in December 1989.

Subsequent missions included 1,271 performed during Operation Desert Storm in 1991.

A dramatic front view of the Nighthawk showing its unique angular construction.

Opposite: The futuristic shape of the highly
successful F-117A Nighthawk.

Below: An F-117 on a daylight reconnaissance
mission.

Specification

First prototype: 18 June 1981
Current users: USA
Crew: Pilot
Wing span: 13.2 m
Length: 20.09 m
Height: 3.78 m
Max take-off weight: 23,814 kg
Max weapon load: See text
Maximum speed: 1,040 km/h
Maximum range: 1,111 km

McDonnell Douglas A-4 Skyhawk USA

Skyhawk was designed to a 1952 requirement of the US Navy for a turbojet attack aircraft to replace the piston-engined Skyraider carried on-board aircraft carriers. The official requirement was for a 13,600 kg gross weight, but the Douglas team led by Ed Heinemann set this aside and, after examining the type of close air support and battlefield interdiction missions then being flown in Korea, came up with an aircraft soon to be nicknamed "Heinemann's Hot Rod". It was a masterly concept, about half the specified weight, uncomplicated, possessing very high speed from a single J65 engine, and with low aspect ratio delta wings with rounded tips of such small dimensions that wing folding for deck-lifts and stowage was unnecessary.

First production A4D-1s (later redesignated A-4As) joined the US Navy in 1956, with higher-powered and heavier versions following for both the Navy and US Marine Corps, and subsequently exported.

Production came to an end in 1979 after 2,960 aircraft, a total which included over 550 two-seaters for combat and training. Those remaining with the US Navy/USMC are almost exclusively for training purposes, but combat versions continue with six other nations, some as upgraded ex-US aircraft and all except for the Argentine A-4M and Ps operating exclusively from land.

Current operating nations are Argentina, Indonesia (E plus two-seaters), Israel (H and N plus two-seaters), Kuwait (KU plus two-seaters), New Zealand (K plus two-seaters) and Singapore (A-4S-1/SU Super Skyhawks). All incorporate very significant upgrading, an example being Singapore's Super Skyhawk with some structural work, new 48.93 kN General Electric F404-GE-100D turbofan engine, modern avionics including head-up and head-down displays, and installation of a flight refuelling probe.

Armament choices can be Maverick missiles, free-fall or smart bombs, rockets and other weapons carried on four underwing and one underfuselage pylons, plus two cannon in the wingroots.

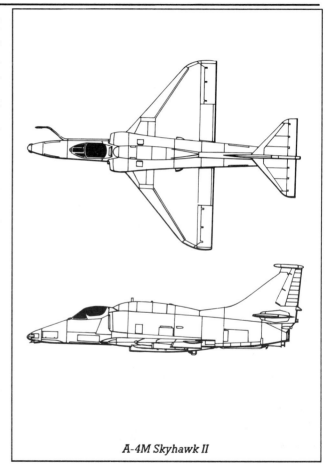

A-4M Skyhawk II

Specification

(Super Skyhawk, where appropriate)

First prototype: 22 June 1954
Current users: See text
Crew: Pilot
Wing span: 8.382 m
Length: 12.7 m
Height: 4.57 m
Empty weight: 4,650 kg

Max take-off weight: 10,200 kg
Max weapon load: See text
Maximum speed: 1,128 km/h
Maximum rate of climb: 3,325 m per minute
Service ceiling: 12,190 m
Maximum range: 1,160 km

Upgraded Israeli Skyhawk.

McDonnell Douglas F-4 Phantom II

One of the most important military aircraft of all time, the **F-4** was originally conceived as a single-seat naval attack-fighter possessing long-range, twin engines for very high performance, and fire-control radar for all-weather operation. However, full development for the US Navy from 1955 led to greater emphasis on fleet air defence, with main armament of six Sparrow medium-range air-to-air missiles, while a second crew member was introduced as a weapon systems/radar officer.

The prototype **F4H-1** first flew on 27 May 1958, and the first production version entered US Navy service from late 1960, known as **F-4A** from 1962 under the new designation system.

The **F-4A** introduced outer-wing dihedral, anhedral tailplane and blown flaps, and a small number were used for trials pending delivery from 1961 of the first major version, which became the **F-4B** for the USN and USMC.

Meanwhile, following trials by the USAF, the **F-4C** was ordered as a land-based tactical fighter, with changes kept to a minimum but still including more powerful examples of the General Electric J79 turbojets, dual controls, inertial navigation, new radar, provision for a large attack weapon load and a new bombing system, wider low-pressure tyres, boom instead of drogue in-flight refuelling capability, and more besides. **F-4C**s entered USAF service from 1963, followed by the RF-4C reconnaissance model in 1964

Experience in Vietnam showed that reliance on missiles alone for air-to-air combat was a mistake, and the **F-4E** multi-role version that entered service from 1967 was given a 20 mm M61A1 Vulcan cannon under the nose and new AN/APQ-120 radar.

Power came from two 79.62 kN with afterburning J79-GE-17A turbojets. Ideally suited to fighter, close air support and interdiction roles, the **F-4E** is today the most important version remaining in service,

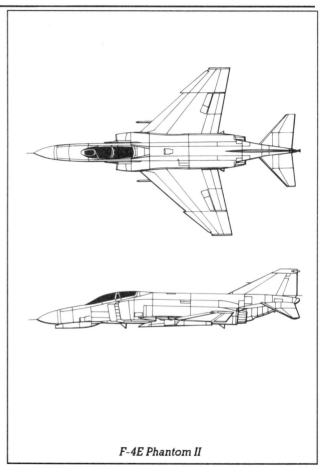

F-4E Phantom II

also having been built by Mitsubishi of Japan as the **F-4EJ**.

Germany received similar aircraft but with leading-edge slats for improved manoeuvrability, as **F-4Fs**.

US **F-4** production ended in 1979, after 5,057 aircraft of all versions.

Although of only minor use today in the USA (with the USAF), **F-4s** remain principal combat aircraft with several foreign air forces, all land based, and a number of important upgrade programmes have kept **F-4s** fully combat capable, including those programmes developed in Germany, Israel and Japan. German **F-4Fs**, for example, have had airframe life extensions, can now launch the latest AMRAAM air-to-air missiles, and new avionics include APG-65GY pulse-Doppler multi-function radar.

An Israeli F-4 Phantom exhibiting its weaponry.

Opposite: German F-4F launching an *AMRAAM.*

Specification
(F-4E where appropriate)

First prototype: See text
Current users: Egypt (E), Germany (F), Greece (R and RF-4E), Iran (D, E and RF-4E), Israel, Japan (F-4EJ Kai and RF-4EJ), South Korea (D, E and RF-4C), Spain (RF-4C), Turkey (E and RF-4E), and USA (F-4G Advanced Wild Weasel to detect and attack radar sites and RF-4C)
Crew: Two
Wing span: 11.71 m

Length: 19.18 m
Height: 4.98 m
Empty weight: 13,756 kg
Max take-off weight: 28,030 kg
Max weapon load: 7,257 kg
Maximum speed: over Mach 2
Maximum rate of climb: 1,880 m per minute
Service ceiling: over 18,290 m
Maximum range: 1,146 km radius of action for interdiction

Below: First flight of re-engined F-4 with twin Pratt and Whitney 1120 power plants.

McDonnell Douglas F-15E Eagle

USA

On 27 July 1972 the prototype **F-15** Eagle first flew as a new air superiority fighter with attack capability. Subsequent production of **F-15A** single-seaters and **F-15B** two-seat operational trainers replaced F-4 Phantoms within the USAF from the mid-1970s, followed by improved **F-15C**s and **D**s. Exports went to Israel, Japan (also still locally built by Mitsubishi) and Saudi Arabia.

On 11 December 1986 the first production **F-15E** two-seater flew, intended to fully exploit both the air-to-air and attack capability of the Eagle in equal measure as a dual-role combat aircraft. Principal changes were directed towards strengthening the airframe structure to permit an enormous increase in maximum take-off weight from 30,844 kg for the F-15C to 36,740 kg for the **F-15E**, simplifying maintenance and improving reliability, and to allow 9g manoeuvres at combat weight throughout the entire flight envelope.

A visual difference became the enlarged canopy over the tandem cockpits. Internal fuel tankage was slightly reduced, however, at 7,643 litres (F-15C has 7,836 litres), and the auxiliary Conformal Fuel Tanks (CFTs) on the air intake sides were also given less capacity at 5,509 litres (F-15C has 5,542 litres).

The CFTs themselves carry twelve of the available weapon attachment points (six each), while the remaining six pylons are positioned as one under each wing, one under each intake and two under the fuselage. The wing and underfuselage pylons can adopt multiple ejectors, thereby increasing the number of individual weapons attached. For example, a single wing pylon can carry two Sidewinder air-to-air missiles in addition to four bombs. The starboard wing 20 mm six-barrel cannon is retained. Pylon weapon choices are enormous, ranging from 907 kg conventional bombs or nuclear bombs to air-to-ground missiles or 8 air-to-air missiles (including AMRAAMs).

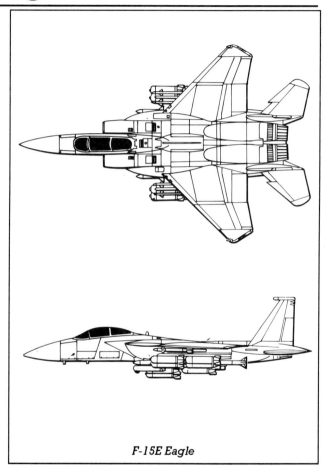

F-15E Eagle

Naturally, the AN/APG-70 radar has both air-to-ground and air-to-air modes, while one LANTIRN pod has forward-looking infra-red (FLIR) and terrain-following radar for navigation by day or night, and the other pod has tracking FLIR and a laser designator for targeting.

Engines are two Pratt & Whitney F100-PW-220 or 229 turbofans, each F100-PW-229 offers 129.45 kN with afterburning.

The USAF has received well over 200 **F-15E**s, and during the Gulf conflict **F-15E**s maintained almost a 96% mission capable rate.

Right: *Dorsal view of a USAF F-15E Eagle.*

__Opposite:__ F-15E Eagles of the Saudi Arabian Air Force on desert patrol.

Specification

First prototype: See text
Current users: Israel (F-15I), Saudi Arabia (F-15S) and USA
Crew: Two
Wing span: 13.05 m
Length: 19.45 m
Height: 5.63 m
Empty weight: 14,515 kg
Max take-off weight: 36,740 kg
Max weapon load: 11,113 kg
Maximum speed: Mach 2.5
Service ceiling: 18,290 m
Maximum range: 4,445 km.

__Below:__ The F-15E Eagle is landing!

McDonnell Douglas F/A-18 Hornet   USA

The **Hornet** was developed out of the Northrop YF-17 which had been in competition with the YF-16 to meet the USAF's lightweight fighter requirement. McDonnell Douglas proposed a navalised variant of the YF-17 to meet a US Navy requirement, for which it would be prime contractor and Northrop the main sub-contractor, while Northrop remained prime contractor on a land-based variant which, in the event, did not attract orders. Indeed, these **Hornets** later exported for land use by air forces are all of the naval model, retaining wing folding.

The original proposal was to develop two versions for the US Navy and US Marine Corps, the F-18 to replace naval F-4 Phantom fighters and the A-18 to replace Vought A-7 Corsair II attack aircraft. However, so close were the two models that a single multi-role variant was developed instead as the **F/A-18**, capable of performing fighter/air superiority, attack, close air support, day/night interdiction and escort roles with equal ability. Moreover, the aircraft could provide its own defence against air attack and, having released its attack weapons, could adopt a full fighter role.

F/A-18A single-seaters and **F/A-18B** two-seat operational trainers entered service from 1983, followed by **F/A-18C**s from 1987 that introduced upgraded avionics plus AMRAAM and infra-red Maverick missiles among new weapon options. The 139th **F/A-18C** was the first **Hornet** with full night attack capability, entering service in 1989.

From 1992 two 78.73 kN with afterburning General Electric F404-GE-402 turbofans became the standard power plant (replacing 71.17 kN F404-GE-400s). Further improvement came in 1994, when the AN/APG-73 radar superseded AN/APG-65, and this radar is now being retrofitted to earlier aircraft.

The very latest **Hornet** variants are the single-seat **F/A-18E** and two-seat F, featuring 97.86 kN with afterburning F414-GE-400 engines, increased fuel load, 8,050 kg weapon load on eleven

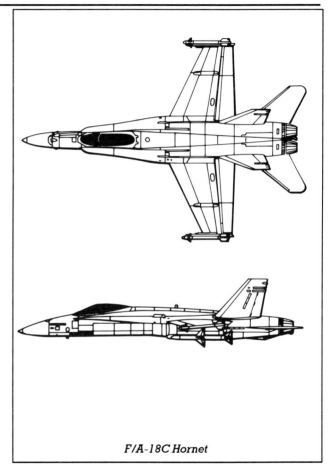

F/A-18C Hornet

pylons instead of 6,214 kg load on nine pylons, updated cockpit, increased wing area, larger leading-edge extensions, and many other changes.

The first **F/A-18E** appeared in September 1995 and the USN/USMC expect to receive about 1,000 by the year 2015.

The current USN/USMC force comprises over 900 **Hornets** operated by 22 and 16 squadrons respectively.

A brace of US Marine Corps Hornets. In the foreground is the two-seat D model and behind, the single-seat C model, flying near the Naval Air Station at Fallon, Nevada.

Opposite: *F/A-18C with port wing Sidewinder and smart bomb.*

Specification
(F/A-18C, as appropriate)

First prototype: See text
Current users: Australia, Canada, Spain, Finland, Kuwait, Malaysia, Switzerland and USA.
Crew: Pilot
Wing span: 11.43 m without wingtip Sidewinder missiles
Length: 17.07 m
Height: 4.66 m
Empty weight: 10,810 kg
Max take-off weight: 25,400 kg
Max weapon load: See text

Maximum speed: over Mach 1.8
Service ceiling: 15,240 m
Maximum range: 1,018 km radius of action

Below: *Battle-ready F/A18E awaiting take-off checks.*

McD. Douglas Defender & Combat Explorer   USA

On 27 February 1963 the prototype first flew of a small observation helicopter for the US Army, which in service became the Hughes OH-6A Cayuse. A civil five-seat derivative followed, produced from 1968 as the Model 500, which in turn spawned various para-military, anti-submarine, armed scout and anti-tank versions for export under the generic name **Defender**, with weapons and sensors appropriate to the chosen task.

Meanwhile, a number of US Army OH-6As were converted into AH-6, EH-6 and MH-6 models for use by the 160th Special Operations Aviation Regiment of the US Army, with weapon combinations/choices including Stinger air-to-air missiles, and some became night vision equipped. More recently, these Special Operations types have been supplemented or replaced by newly built models based on contemporary versions of the MD 500/530.

The current civil versions of the helicopter are the MD-500E with an Allison 250-C20B or R turboshaft engine, derated to 280 kW, and the MD 530F hot and high version with larger rotors and a 250-C30 engine derated to 317 kW. The unarmed or lightly armed para-military and military equivalent of either of these is the **MG Defender**, though TOW 2 anti-armour missiles and sighting system, FLIR, laser ranger and other equipment are optional. However, a specialised anti-armour version is the **TOW Defender**, with four missiles. Nightfox is a variant for night use.

Following earlier trials with a modified OH-6A, in 1990 the MD 520N appeared. This was a radical modification of the MD 500 type, with the traditional anti-torque tail rotor replaced by a NOTAR (no tail rotor) system in which low-pressure air forced out of slots in the tailboom and a direct-jet thruster provide anti-torque forces, both using air produced by an enclosed fan. A Defender version has been developed, and some US Army AH/MH-6s have been converted to

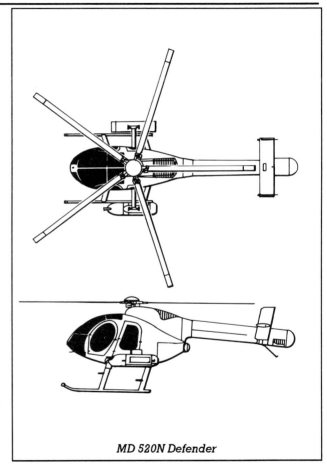

MD 520N Defender

NOTARs.

The very latest armed military helicopter in McDonnell Douglas's expanded series is the new larger eight-seat **Combat Explorer**, a NOTAR type with two 485 kW Pratt & Whitney Canada PW206A or 478 kW Turbomeca Arrius 2C turboshafts, and with many options including a NightHawk electro-optical surveillance and targeting system, FLIR, and Hellfire anti-armour missiles or other weapons.

Production deliveries could begin in 1997.

Combat Explorer with 19-tube 70 mm rocket pod, chin-mounted FLIR, and roof-mounted NightHawk.

Specification
(Combat Explorer, where appropriate)

First prototype: See text
Current users: Defender operators have
    included Argentina, Colombia, Iraq,
    Israel, Kenya, North Korea, South
    Korea, Philippines, and the USA
Crew: Two for attack
Rotor diameter: 10.34 m
Length: 11.84 m
Height: 3.66 m
Empty weight: 1,481 kg
Max take-off weight: 3,130 kg
Max weapon load: See text
Maximum speed: 278 km/h maximum
permitted
Maximum rate of climb: 700 m per
minute
Service ceiling: 6,100 m
Hovering ceiling in ground effect:
3,840 m
Hovering ceiling out of ground effect:
3.260 m
Maximum range: 540 km

*Opposite: The newest Warrior in the
McDonnel Douglas MD Explorer range is the
versatile twin-turbine Combat explorer,
which can be easily configured for utility,
medevac or combat assignments.*

*Right: A Philippine McDonnell Douglas
500MG Defender with rocket launchers.*

McDonnell Douglas AH-64 Apache USA

Originally the Hughes Model 77, **Apache** was conceived to meet a US Army requirement for a heavy attack helicopter capable of day, night and poor weather missions against enemy armour, able to self-deploy using external fuel tanks and operate away from base for extended periods at the front line. A 30 mm automatic Chain Gun was specified as fixed armament, and in 1976 Hellfire missiles were chosen to be the principal anti-armour weapons, with up to sixteen carried on the four stub-wing pylons, although alternative armament could be a maximum of seventy-six 2.75 in rockets or a mix of both, plus stub-tip air-to-air missiles.

First flown as a prototype on 30 September 1975, the YAH-64 was matched against the rival Bell YAH-63 and was chosen for production in late 1976. A total of 821 **AH-64A Apaches** was delivered to the US Army from 1984, each with two 1,171 kW General Electric T700-GE-701 turboshaft engines driving a four-blade main rotor with swept tips and a 'scissors' tail rotor. Extensive avionics include the TADS (target acquisition and designation sight) operated by the gunner to detect and laser-designate a target using any combination of optical, TV and FLIR sensors, while the PNVS (pilot night vision sensor) offers thermal imaging to permit nap-of-the-earth flying in darkness. Both TADS and PNVS are mounted at the nose.

On 15 April 1992 the prototype **AH-64D Longbow Apache** first flew, though on this occasion without the mast-mounted Longbow fire control radar that is the most important feature of this version. Longbow allows up to 256 potential targets to be detected, classified and displayed after just a thirty second radar burst before remasking. Power for **AH-64D** is provided by 1,409 kW T700-GE-701C turboshafts, and substantial upgrading of the avionics enhances capability, reliability and crew efficiency. In a programme to last from 1996 until 2010, all remaining US Army, National Guard and Reserve AH-64As are being modified into **AH-64Ds**, while newly built aircraft were ordered in 1995 by the Netherlands and the UK, the latter for construction by Westland.

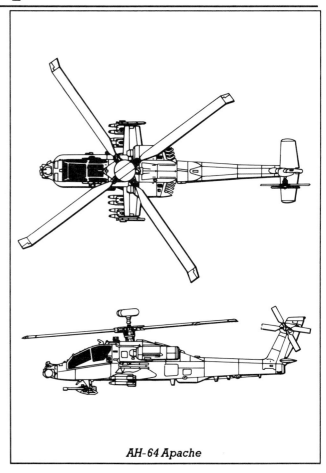

AH-64 Apache

Specification

First prototype: See text
Current users: Egypt (AH-64A),
    Greece (AH-64A), Israel (AH-64A),
    Kuwait (expected), Netherlands
    (AH-64D), Saudi Arabia (AH-64A),
    UK (AH-64D), United Arab Emirates
    (AH-64A) and USA (AH-64A and D)
Crew: Two
Main rotor diameter: 14.63 m
Length: 17.73 m with rotors turning
Height: 4.95 m
Empty weight: 5,352 kg
Max take-off weight: 10,107 kg for ferry
flights
Max weapon load: See text
Maximum speed: 265 km/h
Maximum rate of climb: 942 m per min.
Hovering ceiling in ground effect:
4,115 m
Hovering ceiling out of ground effect:
2,990 m
Maximum range: 433 km without
external tanks

Right: *The second US Army AH-64D Longbow
prototype undergoing flight tests near the
McDonnell Douglas Helicopter Co. facility
in Mesa, Arizona.*

Mikoyan-Gurevich MiG-17   Russia

Even before the MiG-15 was to arrest western complacency in the skies over Korea and prove that the Soviet Union could produce fighters capable of matching and or even surpassing opposing jets for performance, Mikoyan-Gurevich had completed the I-330 prototype in December 1949 of its follow-on design that would first fly on 13 January 1950 and eventually lead to the **MiG-17**.

The similarity in general layout between the longer **MiG-17** and the earlier MiG-15, with its barrel fuselage and nose air intake, swept mid-mounted wings and high tailplane, belied major differences that would take the new MiG beyond its intended very high subsonic speed to become the first Soviet series-produced aircraft to demonstrate supersonic flight. This was first achieved by pilot Ivaschenko on 6 February 1950. Most importantly, the sharply swept wings were of new design, of thinner section and with varying angles of leading-edge sweepback and three boundary-layer fences per wing.

Code named Fresco by NATO, the initial MiG-17A day fighter was followed from 1953 by the MiG-17F (Fresco-C) with a more powerful 33.83 kN Klimov VK-1A turbojet engine, though still for day use.

MiG-17PF introduced a measure of all-weather capability by the adoption of radar.

It is believed that almost 9,000 MiG-17s were built in the Soviet Union, with many more produced in China (as the Shenyang J-5, and also exported), Czechoslovakia and Poland.

Despite its age and limited capability, the MiG-17F remains an important fighter-bomber with many air forces, though not with the producer countries except for China.

Armed with one 37 mm and two 23 mm cannon or three 23 mm cannon, it can carry rocket packs (including air-to-air) or light bombs on the four underwing pylons.

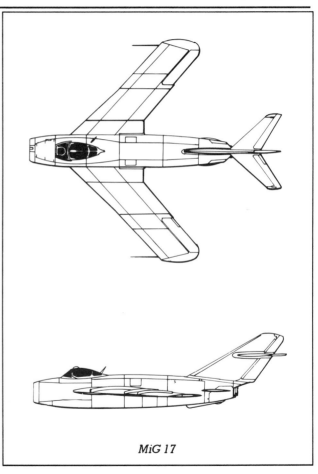

MiG 17

Specification

First prototype: See text
Current users: Afghanistan, Algeria, Angola, Congo, Cuba, Ethiopia, Guinea, Guinea-Bissau, Madagascar, Mali, Mongolia, Romania, Somalia, Syria, Vietnam and Yemen. Includes countries using MiG-17s for training.
Crew: Pilot
Wing span: 9.6 m
Length: 11.36 m
Height: 3.8 m

Max take-off weight: 5,340 kg typically
Max weapon load: 500 kg
Maximum speed: 1,145 km/h
Maximum rate of climb: 3,900 m per minute
Service ceiling: 16,500 m
Maximum range: 1,340 km

MiG Mi-17 grounded for maintenance.

Mikoyan MiG-27   Russia

In June 1967 the 23-11 prototype of the latest Mikoyan fighter, the MiG-23, appeared. Between 1969 and 1985 a total of 5,047 production aircraft were completed in the Soviet Union as Mikoyan's first and only production variable-geometry (swing wing) fighter. Amongst this total, however, were two versions built from 1971 that were not intended for fighter roles, the MiG-23B and BN (NATO named Flogger-F). These were employed instead for ground attack, with the nose radar replaced by appropriate attack systems. No longer in Soviet service, but possibly kept in strategic reserve, some exported aircraft remain operational.

Even before MiG-23B/BN appeared, Mikoyan had started development of a fully dedicated ground attack aircraft based on the MiG-23 basic design, of such difference that a new designation was subsequently issued, as **MiG-27**. The most obvious change was that the rounded nosecone housing the MiG-23 fighter's radar was replaced by a new sloping nose without radar, giving the pilot an improved downward view. Steel armour was attached to the outside of the cockpit for protection from ground fire and the air intakes became non-variable. Other features included a stronger undercarriage , new wing and flap control, wingroot extensions, PrNK-23 nav/attack system, and a laser rangefinder/optical sighting system/target designator. The Soyuz R-29B-300 engine was given a two-position nozzle and offered 112.78 kN with afterburning.

The **MiG-27** first joined Soviet units in 1973, having originally been designated MiG-23BM, and production of over 900 lasted ten years. The most sophisticated production version was the MiG-27K (Flogger-D), of which some 200 were built and were further improved during the early 1980s by upgrading to MiG-27D (Flogger-J) standard, but these are no longer in service. India became a MiG-23BN operator, and in 1983 MiG-27 production was initiated in that country, based around the simplified MiG-27M (Flogger-J). The first Indian MiG-27M was built from Soviet components and appeared in 1986, while MiG-27L Bahadurs of all-Indian manufacture came off Hindustan Aeronautics Ltd production lines from 1988. Production by HAL lasted until 1994, and today that nation is the only MiG-27 operator.

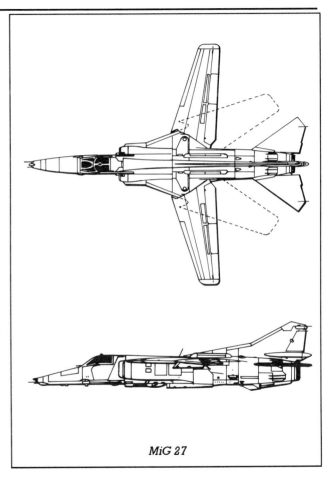

MiG 27

Specification

First prototype: See text
Current users: India
Crew: Pilot
Wing span: 13.965 m spread, and
7.779 m sweptback
Length: 17.076 m
Height: 5 m
Empty weight: 12,100 kg
Max take-off weight: 20,670 kg
Max weapon load: 3,000 kg normally
Typical weapon load: Weapons on
seven pylons can include laser-guided
and other missiles, guns, munition
dispensers and TV-guided bombs, but
not laser-guided bombs. Four R-60
Aphid air-to-air missiles can be carried
for self defence.
Maximum speed: Mach 1.7
Maximum rate of climb: 12,000 m per
minute
Service ceiling: 14,000 m
Maximum range: 2,500 km with three
drop tanks

Spectacular view of Indian-built MiG-27L Bahadur.

Mil Mi-8 and Mi-17 Russia

One of the most successful helicopters of all time, the **Mi-8** first flew on 24 June 1961 as a turboshaft-powered replacement for the piston-engined Mi-4. At that time the **Mi-8** was fitted with just one engine, an Ivchenko AI-24V; on 2 August 1962 a twin Isotov TV2-117-engined prototype made a hovering flight and this became the standard engine layout for production **Mi-8**s that left the factories from 1965.

Given the code name Hip by NATO, the **Mi-8** remains in production and many thousands have been delivered to military and civil operators in Russia/Soviet Union and some 57 other countries. The cabin is large enough for 28 passengers or other loads, with access made easy by the use of clamshell rear loading doors. In military guise, the **Mi-8**'s roles can include armed assault, close air support, fire suppression, minelaying, airborne command post, reconnaissance and electronic warfare. The Mi-8TV Hip-C is an armed assault version of 1968 first appearance, based on the Mi-8T transport and carrying 24 troops plus four 57 mm rocket packs or bombs on outriggers when required. The improved Mi-8TB Hip-E of 1975 appearance carries six rocket packs and four AT-2 Skorpion (Swatter) anti-tank missiles plus a 12.7 mm machine-gun; Mi-8TBK Hip-F for export increases missile armament to six AT-3 Malyutkas (Saggers). The current engine arrangement is two 1,119 kW TV2-117AGs.

In 1976 the Mi-18 prototype first flew, based on the **Mi-8** but with TV3-117 engines. Production versions reverted to Mi-8 designations for Russian/Soviet use and Mi-17 when exported. With the option of six extra troops, current armed versions include the Mi-8MT Hip-H with 1,417 kW TV3-117MT turboshafts and the Mi-8MTV for use in hot and high conditions. Typical armament on six outrigger pylons comprises four 80 mm rocket packs and/or UPK-23 gun packs, or other weapons including submunition dispensers, plus a pintle gun in the doorway. The very latest models include the Mi-17MD for 36-40 troops, exhibited at the 1995 Paris Air Show.

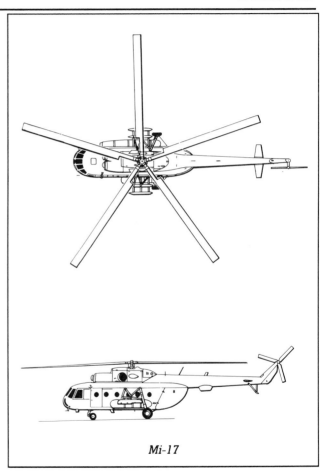

Mi-17

Specification

(Hip-C)

First prototype: See text
Current users: See text
Crew: Two pilots and a flight engineer
Main rotor diameter: 21.288 m
Length: 25.244 m with rotors turning
Height: 5.654 m
Empty weight: 7,260 kg
Max take-off weight: 12,000 kg
Max weapon load: See text
Maximum speed: 250 km/h
Service ceiling: 4,500 m
Hovering ceiling in ground effect: 1,800 m
Hovering ceiling out of ground effect: 850 m
Maximum range: 425-520 km typically

Mi-8MT Hip-H with weapon outrigger pylons. (Piotr Butowski).

Mil Mi-24, Mi-25 and Mi-35   Russia

The **Mi-24** was the Soviet Union's first purpose designed helicopter gunship to enter mass production, it carried eight assault troops and thereby became a much bulkier helicopter than its American counterparts. Indeed, the earliest production versions had conventional cockpits with side-by-side seating for the flight crew. However, operational experience indicated that a radical rethink of the crew arrangement was necessary to fulfil the helicopter's full potential as a gunship and the **Mi-24D** (NATO code name Hind-D) of 1976 appearance incorporated separate tandem cockpits for the pilot and weapon system operator, though still retaining the troop cabin and a jump seat for a mechanic. Other **Mi-24** versions followed with various armament and systems changes, plus some very specialised models for unarmed artillery radiation reconnaissance, spotting/reconnaissance, and nuclear/biological/chemical sampling; **Mi-24D** was the main production version within the total of over 2,300 **Mi-24s** and derivatives built from 1970-1989. Principal armament for **Mi-24D** is a four-barrel 12.7 mm gun under the nose and AT-2 Skorpion (Swatter) anti-tank missiles associated with the Falanga-V system. Current CIS forces deploy about 1,250 **Mi-24s**.

Power for **Mi-24s** built after 1972 comes from two Isotov TV3-117 turboshafts. The TV3-117VMs in the **Mi-24V** Hind-E are each rated at 1,659 kW. It was the **Mi-24V** that introduced the improved Shturm-V anti-tank system with electro-optical sight under the nose and associated AT-6 Kokon (Spiral) anti-tank missiles carried beneath the stub-wing tips and on two of the four stub-wing pylons (typically eight missiles, but 12 possible). Other **Mi-24V** weapon options can include rocket and cannon packs, Strela, Igla or R-60 (Aphid) air-to-air missiles, or submunition dispensers up to a weight of 1,200 kg. **Mi-24VP**, Hind-E variant, has a 23 mm cannon in place of the earlier machine-gun. **Mi-25** became the designation for exported **Mi-24Ds** to Third World countries, while **Mi-35/35P** are the export designations for **Mi-24V** and **P** models. The proposed upgrade of Hinds to a new **Mi-35M** (Russian **Mi-24VM**) standard was recently revealed, to offer major upgrade of the avionics and anti-tank system.

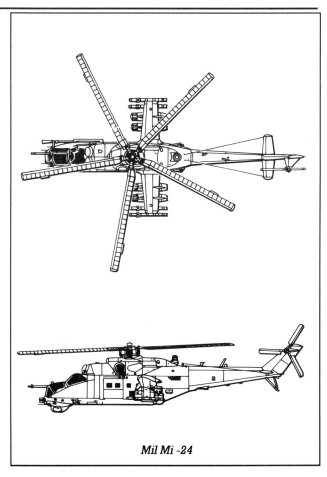

Mil Mi -24

Specification
(Mi-24V as appropriate)

First prototype: 19 September 1969 (Mi-24)
Crew: 2, see text
Main rotor diameter: 17.3 m
Length: 21.35 m with rotors turning
Height: 5.47 m
Empty weight: 8,340 kg

Current users: Afghanistan, Algeria, Angola, Cambodia, Chad, CIS, Cuba, Czech Republic, Ethiopia, India, Iran, Iraq, North Korea, Libya, Mozambique, Nicaragua, Peru, Poland, Slovakia, Sri Lanka, Syria and Yemen.
Max take-off weight: 11,800 kg
Max weapon load: See text

Maximum speed: 335 km/h
Service ceiling: 4,600 m
Hovering ceiling out of ground effect: 2,000 m
Maximum range: 450 km typically

Mi-24V Hind E (Piotr Butowski).

119

Mil Mi-28 Russia

While Mi-24 production was in full flow, in 1980, Mil initiated the design of a new attack helicopter with emphasis on weapon carrying, the two crew occupying tandem stepped cockpits and with no separate bulky cabin for assault troops (a hatch in the fuselage side of **Mi-28** permits transportation of two or three persons or cargo should the need arise, or for the extraction of standed crews in a battle zone). The first experimental helicopter flew on 10 November 1982, but it was not until 1988 that the first of two new representative prototypes appeared. Delays have meant that early production **Mi-28**s have only recently entered service with the Russian forces, and have been followed by the prototype of the Mi-28N all-weather, day/night version with mast-mounted millimetre-wave radar and a search/targeting unit with optical, TV and thermal modes.

Power for the **Mi-28** (NATO code name Havoc) comes from two 1,659 kW Isotov TV3-117VMA turboshaft engines, fitted with infra-red suppression cool air mixers, and driving a five-blade composites main rotor with elastomeric bearings and two separate two-blade tail rotors in 'scissors' form. The engines are separated and mounted low to assist survivability. The armoured crew cockpits can withstand hits from up to 12.7 mm ammunition or 20 mm fragments, while 12 m per second vertical landings can be survived through undercarriage and airframe features.

Mi-28 has the PrPNK-28 weapon, flight and navigation system, allowing nap-of-the-earth flight at just 15 m height above the ground. A KOPS electro-optical system is used to identify and track targets and establish the best engagement position, and functions with the laser rangefinder, the pilot's helmet target designator, and undernose 30 mm cannon. Four stub-wing pylons offer a 2,000 kg weapon load, typically sixteen AT-6 Kokon (Spiral) anti-tank missiles of the Shturm-V or 9M120 missiles of the Ataka-V system. Other armament can be the usual mix of rockets (up to 122 mm), cannon pods, submunition dispensers, bombs, etc.

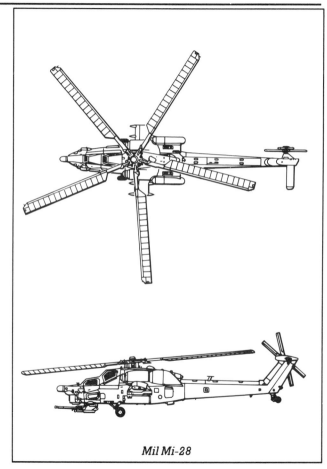

Mil Mi-28

Specification

First prototype: See text
Current users: Russia
Crew: Two
Main rotor diameter: 17.2 m
Length: 21.155 m with rotors turning
Height: 4.7 m
Empty weight: 8,095 kg
Max take-off weight: 11,660 kg
Max weapon load: See text
Maximum speed: 300 km/h
Maximum rate of climb: 816 m per minute
Service ceiling: 5,800 m
Hovering ceiling out of ground effect: 3,600 m
Maximum range: 460 km typically

Mi-28, showing the optical sight, laser rangefinder/designator and 30 mm cannon. The 300 rounds of ammunition in two containers move with the cannon to dispense with flexible feed chutes.

Mitsubishi F-1 Japan

Having flown the prototype T-2 two-seat trainer in 1971 as Japan's first-ever indigenous supersonic aircraft, the decision was made in the following year to develop a single-seat close air support derivative.

For trials, two early production T-2s were converted into prototypes, both making their first flights in mid-1975. After a lengthy trials period with the JASDF's Air Proving Wing, production of the single-seater was given the go-ahead in late 1976 and the designation **F-1** issued.

Powered by two Ishikawajima-Harima TF40-IHI-801A turbofans, basically licence-built Rolls-Royce Turbomeca Adour Mk 801As and each rated at 32.5 kN with afterburning, the **F-1** joined the JASDF from 1977. Production rate was slow, however, and the last of seventy-seven was not delivered until March 1987.

The **F-1** will continue in service until replaced by the FS-X in the next century.

Mitsubishi Electric produced the **F-1**'s J/AWG-12 radar carried in the nose, which has both air-to-air and air-to-ground modes, together with the head-up display, and the J/ASQ-1 fire control system and bombing computer that superseded the original system from 1982 to allow the F-1 to carry and launch two Mitsubishi ASM-1 air-to-surface missiles.

Other weapons up to a total weight of 2,720 kg can include rockets and bombs on the single underfuselage and four underwing pylons, with multiple ejector racks increasing the number of individual weapons carried. Fixed armament is a 20 mm cannon. For an air-to-air role, **F-1** can activate wingtip launchers for Sidewinder missiles, with two more carried under the outer wing pylons.

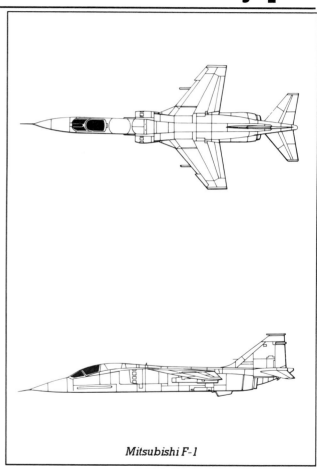

Mitsubishi F-1

Specification

First prototype: 16 June 1977 for a production F-1
Current users: Japan
Crew: Pilot
Wing span: 7.88 m
Length: 17.85 m
Height: 4.48 m
Empty weight: 6,358 kg
Max take-off weight: 13,700 kg
Max weapon load: See text
Maximum speed: Mach 1.5
Maximum rate of climb: 10,675 m per minute
Service ceiling: 15,250 m

A flight of camouflaged Mitsubishi F-1s.

Nanchang Q-5   China

Development of the **Q-5** began in 1958 when Shenyang was tasked with producing an attack/strike/close air support aircraft with an armour-protected cockpit, using the Russian Mikoyan MiG-19 fighter as the basic starting technology. At that time the first flight of a Chinese produced MiG-19 (to be designated J-6) was still years off, although technology transfer had occurred through the delivery from Russia of MiG-19s in knock-down form for Chinese assembly. But Shenyang was too heavily committed to the J-6 programme and **Q-5** development was moved to Nanchang. Unfortunately, soon after transfer, the **Q-5** programme was cancelled (in 1961), only to be revived in 1963.

The prototype **Q-5** finally flew on 5 June 1965 but trials indicated a number of problems and series manufacture was further delayed until 1969. The production **Q-5**, released in 1970, showed little external similarity to the MiG, having a lengthened area-ruled fuselage to minimise transonic drag and a pointed nosecone (without radar). An internal bay was incorporated to provide 'clean' accommodation for two 500 kg bombs, with lighter weapons carried under the wings and fuselage when required. Some **Q-5**s subsequently had nuclear capability added. But range was insufficient, and in 1980 the Q-5 I appeared, with a huge increase in fuel tankage by deletion of the bomb bay. To make good the weapon-carrying loss, two more external pylons were added. Fixed armament comprises two 23 mm cannon in the wing roots.

Export of a modified version to Pakistan in 1983, as the A-5C, led to similar adoption of six underwing pylons for subsequent Q types, while prototypes of the later A-5M version produced with assistance from Italy were given eight underwing pylons in addition to the standard four under the fuselage, plus avionics upgrades. The first A-5M appeared in 1988 and Myanmar received the first production examples in 1993. Power for the **Q-5** models is provided by two 31.87 kN with afterburning Liming WP6 turbojets, while A-5s have 39.72 kN with afterburning WP6As which may be available for retrofit to **Q-5**s.

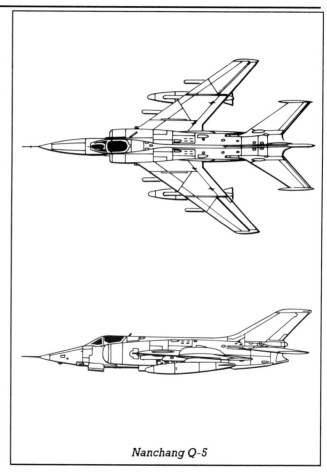

Nanchang Q-5

Specification

(A-5C as appropriate)

First prototype: See text
Current users: Bangladesh, China, Myanmar, North Korea and Pakistan
Crew: Pilot
Wing span: 9.7 m
Length: 16.255 m
Height: 4.516 m
Empty weight: 6,494 kg
Max take-off weight: 12,000 kg
Max weapon load: 2,000 kg

Maximum speed: 1,210 km/h
Maximum rate of climb: 6,180 m per minute
Service ceiling: 15,850 m
Maximum range: 2,000 km

A-5C of No 26 "Black Spiders" Squadron, Pakistan Air Force. (Denis Hughes)

Northrop Grumman F-5

The **F-5** was conceived as a supersonic lightweight tactical fighter of uncomplicated form, with US Government financial backing, for export to foreign nations under the US Military Assistance Program (MAP). A measure of the success is that after flying the N-156 prototype on 30 July 1959, more than 2,600 aircraft of all types were built by Northrop in the USA and under licence in Canada, South Korea, The Netherlands, Spain, Switzerland and Taiwan. Of these, some 1,700 remain operational, and structural/systems/avionics upgrade programmes are underway in Belgium, Canada, Israel, the USA and elsewhere to help ensure combat capability well into the next century.

The original single-seat F-5A Freedom Fighter was built as a Mach 1.4 day fighter, powered by two 18.15 kN afterburning General Electric J85-GE-13 turbojets. In addition to two 20 mm cannon and wingtip Sidewinder air-to-air missiles, five pylons were provided for a 2,812 kg load that usually comprises attack weapons. Original instrumentation was basic, including an optical sight. The two-seat training variant became the F-5B. The first F-5A flew in July 1963 and in February 1965 Iran became the first operator under MAP. A reconnaissance variant is the RF-5A.

On 11 August 1972 the first flight took place of the greatly improved F-5E Tiger II single-seater, again backed by the US Government as an International Fighter Aircraft. Currently the most important F-5 variant, features two J85-GE-21B turbojets developing 22.24 kN with afterburning, pushing the maximum speed to Mach 1.63. Emerson AN/APQ-159 radar was installed to provide all-weather capability while automatic leading-edge flaps enhance manoeuvrability. Weapon load also increased to 3,175 kg. Deliveries started in 1973. A single cannon two-seater is the F-5F, and the RF-5E TigerEye is a reconnaissance model. Optional Tiger II upgrades include AN/APG-66 or other radar, multi-function cockpit displays, head-up display, new computers and much more besides.

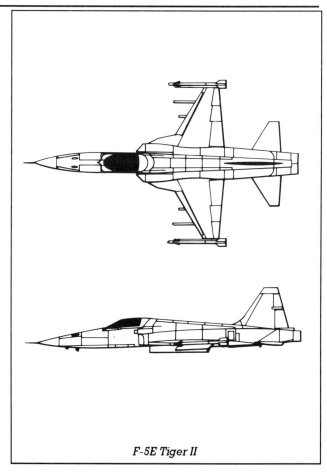

F-5E Tiger II

Specification

(F-5E as appropriate)
First prototype: See text
Current users: Bahrain, Brazil, Canada
(being withdrawn), Chile, Greece,
Honduras, Indonesia, Iran, Jordan,
Kenya, South Korea, Malaysia, Mexico,
Morocco, Norway, Philippines,
Saudi Arabia, Singapore, Switzerland,
Spain, Taiwan, Thailand, Turkey,
Uruguay, USA, Venezuela, Vietnam
and Yemen

Crew: Pilot
Wing span: 8.13 m
Length: 14.68 m
Height: 4.06 m
Empty weight: 4,347 kg
Max take-off weight: 11,192 kg
Max weapon load: See text
Maximum speed: Mach 1.63
Maximum rate of climb: 10,500 m per minute
Service ceiling: 15,800 m
Maximum range: 2,861 km with drop tanks

*Canadian-built F-5A firing rockets, as now
used by Venezuela.*

Panavia Tornado IDS International

The Tornado is a swing-wing combat aircraft available for close air support and battlefield interdiction as well as for the more typical strike and bomber roles.It is the result of an outstandingly successful international programme between Germany, Italy and the UK that started with the formation of Panavia Aircraft in 1969 (originally also including The Netherlands). The Multi-Role Combat Aircraft, as **Tornado** was first named, needed to be capable of transonic flight at sea level, high supersonic speed, have good manoeuvrability and loiter capability, and with substantial range, yet be compact and have acceptable field performance. The pilot and navigator were placed in tandem cockpits, and the chosen power plant comprises two 71.2 kN with afterburning Turbo Union RB199 Mk 103 turbofan engines. Ground mapping radar was installed for blind navigation and targeting, and terrain following radar.

The first prototype flew in Germany on 14 August 1974, followed by British and Italian prototypes, and in June 1979 the RAF and Luftwaffe received their first IDSs. A Tri-national Training Establishment was founded in the UK in 1981 for international crew training, and the RAF began operational deployment in 1982, following the first German Squadron. The first 'export' **Tornado** for Saudi Arabia flew in 1986. A total of 781 IDS types have been ordered and most delivered, including German Navy maritime strike aircraft (some since transferred to the Luftwaffe), more powerful Luftwaffe ECRs (electronic combat and reconnaissance) with specialised equipment, and a second batch of 48 IDSs for Saudi Arabia for delivery by 1997. Apart from the basic GR Mk 1, the RAF deploys GR Mk 1As for reconnaissance and 1Bs for maritime attack. The GR Mk 4/4A represent 142 RAF Mk 1/1As for mid-life upgrade during 1996-2002, receiving FLIR, TIALD, colour multi-function displays and more.

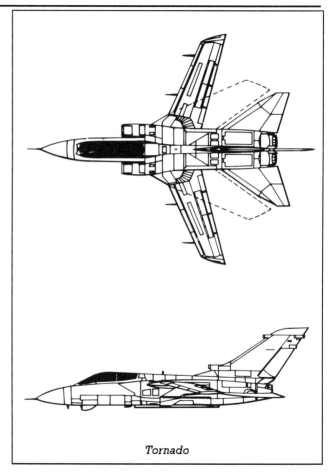

Tornado

Specification

First prototype: See text
Current users: Germany (air force and navy), Italy, Saudi Arabia and the UK. The United Arab Emirates might lease a small number of RAF GR Mk 1s
Crew: Two
Wing span: 13.91 m spread, and 8.6 m sweptback
Length: 16.7 m
Height: 5.95 m
Empty weight: up to 14,500 kg

Max take-off weight: 28,000 kg
Max weapon load: The 9,000 kg weapon load is carried on four swivelling underwing pylons and three underfuselage pylons, with multi-store carriers available to increase the number of individual weapons. Typical weapon loads are eight 1,000 lb bombs plus two Sidewinders for self-defence, or submunition dispensers, or various missiles including Maverick air-to-surface, ALARM or HARM anti-radar, or Sea Eagle or Kormoran

anti-ship. Two 27 mm cannon are standard in all but ECR and reconnaissance versions.
Maximum speed: Mach 1.8 with external weapons/drop tanks or Mach 2.2 without
Service ceiling: over 15,240 m
Maximum range: 1,482 km radius of action with four 1,000 lb bombs, two drop tanks and two Sidewinders

RAF GR Mk 4 development aircraft.

PZL-Swidnik Mi-2   Poland

Although designed in the Soviet Union by Mil and first flown on 22 September 1961, development and production of the **Mi-2** (NATO code name Hoplite) was entrusted to PZL-Swidnik in Poland in 1964, leading to the first Polish example flying in 1965. Amazingly, well over 5,400 examples have been built over the years for a wide variety of military and civil roles, the majority having been delivered to the former Soviet Union and some production continues.

Military versions of the **Mi-2** include specialised versions for mine-laying, smokescreen laying and radiation reconnaissance, airborne command post, land and sea rescue, photographic reconnaissance, transport (8 troops or cargo), medical evacuation and training, but very significant are the armed versions.

The Mi-2URN Zmija first appeared in 1973 armed with two Mars 2 launchers on pylons, each carrying sixteen 57 mm rockets. A version with four pylon-mounted 7.62 mm gun pods plus two further guns in the cabin was the Mi-2US Adder, also of 1973 appearance but thought to be out of service. These were followed in 1976 by the Mi-2URP Salamandra, with four AT-3 Malyutka (Sagger) anti-tank missiles, while the Mi-2URPG Gniewosz added four Gad (Strela 2, AS-7 Grail) air-to-air missiles.

Power for the **Mi-2** comes from two 294 kW PZL-Rzeszów GTD-350 turboshaft engines, driving a three-blade metal main rotor and two-blade tail rotor. The main rotor has flapping, drag and pitch hinges, anti-flutter weights, balance plates and hydraulic dampers.

To increase range, two auxiliary fuel tanks can be attached to the sides of the fuselage.

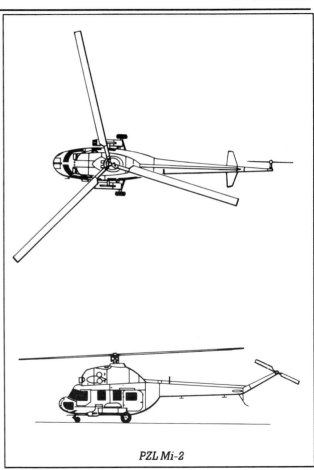

PZL Mi-2

Specification

First prototype: See text
Current users: Military and civil have
  included Bulgaria, Cuba, Czech Republic,
  Djibouti, Egypt, Hungary, Iraq, Latvia,
  Libya, Myanmar, Nicaragua, North Korea,
  Poland, Romania, Russia, Slovakia and
  Syria
Crew: Pilot, or two
Main rotor diameter: 14.5 m
Length: 17.42 m with rotors turning
Height: 3.75 m
Empty weight: up to 2,400 kg
Max take-off weight: up to 3,700 kg
Max weapon load: See text
Cruising speed: 200 km/h
Maximum rate of climb: 270 m per minute
Service ceiling: 4,000 m
Hovering ceiling in ground effect:
2,000 m
Hovering ceiling out of ground effect:
1,000 m
Maximum range: 796 km

One of the 5,400 Polish-built Mi-2s.

Saab 37 Viggen   Sweden

Viggen first flew on 8 February 1967 as a combat aircraft intended for several individual and demanding roles, requiring also extremely good take-off and landing performance to permit the use of major roads as dispersal airstrips. Production deliveries started in February 1971, with the AJ37 attack version. Two years later the first SF37 appeared as the expected photo-reconnaissance **Viggen**, although production deliveries did not begin until 1977, by which time the SH37 for sea surveillance had already entered service. The final combat model was the JA37 interceptor, delivered from 1979 and becoming operational in the following year. The fifth **Viggen** version was the SK37 tandem cockpit trainer. In total, 329 Viggens of all versions went to the Swedish Air Force, the last (a JA37) in June 1990, and Viggens were still operated by 14 Squadrons in 1995. However, in October that year the first **Viggen** pilots began converting to Gripens.

Today the principal **Viggen** attack force is represented by 75 AJS37s, comprising AJ37s, SH37s and SF37s fairly recently modified to undertake any of the attack, interceptor or reconnaissance roles as required. **Viggens** had always been able to offer a secondary role capability, but due to many upgrades the AJS can undertake each mission with equal effectiveness. This has been made possible principally by the installation of a new computer, new mission data entry method, and new reconnaissance system. The computer also permits a wider armament choice, including the DWS39 cluster weapons dispenser and RBS15F anti-ship missile. Stores are carried on four underwing and three underfuselage pylons, while fixed armament comprises a 30 mm cannon.

Viggen introduced the rear-mounted wings and canard configuration to the military scene, an arrangement that has since been widely emulated, selected to offer good handling at all speeds and delay super-stall at high angles of incidence. Power for the aircraft comes from a single Volvo RM8 engine with an augmented rating of 115.7 kN.

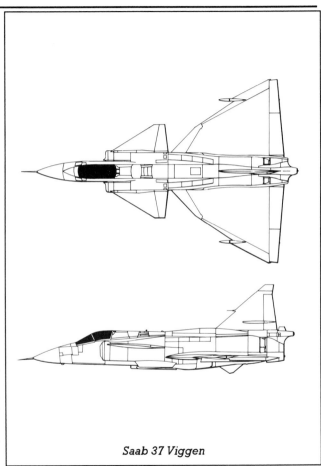

Saab 37 Viggen

Specification

First prototype: See text
Current users: Sweden
Crew: Pilot, except for the SK37
Wing span: 10.6 m
Length: 16.4 m
Height: 5.9 m
Max take-off weight: 20,000 kg
Max weapon load: See text
Maximum speed: over Mach 2
Service ceiling: 18,000 m
Maximum range: 500 km radius of action
for a low-level attack mission

A fully-armed Swedish Air Force Viggen ready for take-off.

Sepecat Jaguar

The Anglo-French **Jaguar** programme began in 1965 to develop a tactical strike fighter and advanced trainer with attack capability suited to transonic speed at low altitude and supersonic flight at height on the power of two Rolls-Royce Turbomeca Adour afterburning turbofans. A starting point for the design was the Breguet Br 121, although Jaguar became a larger and heavier aircraft. Good take-off and landing performance was essential, achieved in part by adoption of efficient wings with full-span double-slotted flaps, leading-edge slats and lateral control spoilers; the navigation and weapon-aiming systems offered the possibility of highly accurate first-pass ground attack.

The first prototype flew on 8 September 1968, it was a French two-seat trainer, followed in 1969 by prototypes of the French and British single-seaters. A French Jaguar E two-seater became the first production aircraft to enter service, in 1972, with the French single-seat Jaguar A becoming operational in mid-1973. For the RAF, the Jaguar B two-seater first flew as a prototype in 1971, and the Jaguar S single-seater entered service in 1974 as the Jaguar GR Mk 1. The latter became Mk 1As when subsequently given inertial navigation systems, and some are currently being further upgraded to Mk 1B standard by the installation of a TIALD pod, wide-angle head-up display, head-down displays, global positioning system and HOTAS. Already many RAF Jaguars had been retrofitted with more powerful Adour Mk 104s, each 35.14 kN with afterburning. The 4,536 kg attack weapon load is carried on four underwing and one underfuselage pylons, while the single-seaters have two fixed 30 mm cannon and the two-seaters just one. An alternative store is a reconnaissance pod.

The export version became the **Jaguar International**, first going to Ecuador in 1977. Internationals have uprated engines and can carry Sidewinder or Magic air-to-air missiles on overwing launch rails, although some other Jaguars can also carry these missiles on wing pylons. Internationals have also been built in India as Shamshers, those assigned for maritime strike being the only radar-equipped examples.

Sepecat Jaguar

Specification

First prototype: See text
Current users: Ecuador, France, Nigeria, Oman and the UK
Crew: Pilot, or two in the trainers
Wing span: 8.69 m
Length: 15.52 m for single-seaters
Height: 4.89 m
Empty weight: 6,985 kg
Max take-off weight: 15,700 kg
Max weapon load: See text
Maximum speed: Mach 1.6

Maximum range: 800 km radius of action with four 1,000 lb bombs

Two differently camouflaged French Air Force Jaguar As (SIRPA "AIR")

Soko J-22 Orao & Avioane IAR-93   Romania/fmr. Yugoslavia

The ambitious Jurom programme by CNIAR (later Avioane) of Romania and Soko of the former Yugoslavia to jointly develop a combat aircraft suited to close air support, attack and reconnaissance, with limited air defence capability, was started in 1970. The first flight of single-seat prototypes in both countries took place on 31 October 1974, followed by two-seat prototypes on 29 January 1977. The first of fifteen pre-production aircraft built in each country flew in 1978.

Although of indigenous design, the aircraft adopted some foreign technologies, including British, French and US avionics, British Rolls-Royce Viper 600 series turbojet engines (licence built), British Martin-Baker ejection seats, Italian undercarriage components, Soviet 23 mm GSh-23L guns (two each), and attack weapons from several countries, including (according to the version) US TV-guided Maverick and Soviet missiles plus French Durandals, to name a few. Attack weapons are carried on four underwing and one underfuselage pylons within the overall weight limits of 2,100 kg for the **IAR-93B** and 2,800 kg for **Orao 2**.

The **IAR-93B** and **Orao 2** in single and two-seat versions are each powered by two 22.37 kN with afterburning turbojets, as Viper Mk 633-47s and 633-41s respectively. It was the protracted development of the afterburners that meant that early production single- and two-seat **IAR-93A**s and **Orao**s had to use 17.66 kN non-afterburning Viper Mk 632s and thereby undertake mostly non-combat roles, although upgrade to **IAR-93B** and **Orao 2** standards has been underway. A specific two-seat reconnaissance version of Orao 2 is known as the NJ-22 Orao 2D. Current operational status is unknown, although Avioane delivered 36 **IAR-93A** and many of the 165 **IAR-93B**s required and Soko delivered 124 **Orao/Orao 2**s before further construction had to be terminated in the former Yugoslavia. It is known that Avioane has stored fuselages and wings.

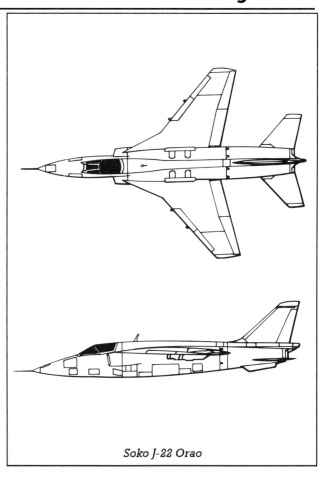

Soko J-22 Orao

Specification

First prototype: See text
Current users: Romania and Serbia
(Yugoslavia)
Crew: One or two
Wing span: 9.3 m
Length: 14.9 m for the single-seater
Height: 4.52 m
Empty weight: 5,500 kg for IAR-93B
and 5,750 kg for Orao 2
Max take-off weight: 10,900 kg for
IAR-93B and 11,080 kg for Orao 2
Max weapon load: See text
Maximum speed: 1,086 km/h
Service ceiling: 13,500 m
Maximum range: 530 km radius of
action with a 1,000 kg weapon load

Soko J-22 Orao refuelling and re-arming.

Sukhoi Su-17, Su-20 and Su-22   Russia

In 1965 a programme was initiated to develop a derivative of the Su-7 attack aircraft with variable-geometry wings. The Su-7IG or S-22I technology demonstrator was first flown on 2 August 1966, with only the outer portion of the wings having variable sweep, leaving large fixed inner sections. Yet the improvement to field performance and payload was substantial, leading to a pre-production prototype that appeared in 1968 as the S-32.

The initial production version of the S-32 was **Su-17** (NATO code name Fitter-B), with a Lyulka AL-7F1-250 turbojet offering 94.15 kN with afterburning, and carrying 2,800 kg of fuel and a 3,000 kg weapon load. Built during 1970-72, it was followed by the far more important Su-17M Fitter-C, the first version to have the 109.84 kN with afterburning AL-21F-3 engine, 3,630 kg of fuel and a 4,000 kg weapon load. The Su-17M2 Fitter-D introduced a laser rangefinder and DISS-7 Doppler navigation radar among other upgrades and was produced up to 1979, while subsequent versions included the definitive Su-17M4 Fitter-K, produced up to 1990 and carrying 4,250 kg of weapons on four underfuselage pylons, four pylons under the inner wing sections, plus two further underwing pylons only for carrying for R-60 (Aphid) air-to-air missiles. Fixed armament comprises two 30 mm cannon in the wing roots. Two-seat training variants have only one cannon.

Su-17M3 and M4 can carry the KKR-1 reconnaissance pod, and the very recent withdrawal of Su-17s from CIS use is intended to leave only reconnaissance versions operational. Export versions of the **Su-17** received **Su-20** and **Su-22** designations, some Su-22 having 112.78 kN with afterburning Soyuz R29BS-300 engines. A proposed upgrade of existing Fitters is the Su-22M5, a prototype of which was displayed at the 1995 Paris Air Show. This has a very extensive avionics upgrade developed in association with French companies, including a Phathom radar in the shock-cone, replacing the Klon-54 laser rangefinder.

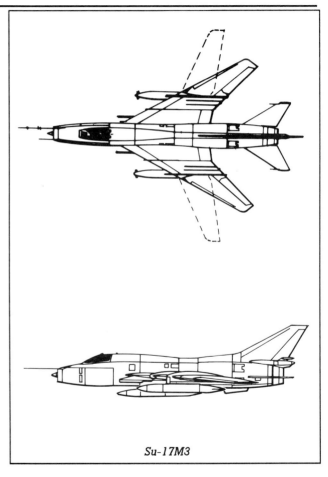

Su-17M3

Specification
(Su-17M4 where appropriate)

First prototype: See text
Current users: Afghanistan (Su-22), Algeria
(Su-20), Angola (Su-22), Czech Republic
(Su-22), Egypt (Su-20), Hungary
(Su-22), Iraq (Su-20), Kazakhstan, Libya
(Su-22), North Korea (Su-22), Peru
(Su-22), Poland (Su-22), Russia, Slovakia
(Su-22), Syria (Su-22), Turkmenistan,
Ukraine, Uzbekistan, Vietnam (Su-22)
and Yemen (Su-22)
Crew: Pilot
Wing span: 13.68 m spread, and 10.025 m
sweptback
Length: 19.02 m
Height: 5.129 m
Empty weight: 10,640 kg
Max take-off weight: 19,500 kg
Max weapon load: See text
Maximum speed: Mach 1.77
Service ceiling: 15,200 m
Maximum range: 2,550 km

Polish Fitters, including Su-22M4 Fitter-K and two-seater. (Piotr Butowski).

Sukhoi Su-25 and Su-25T/TM   Russia

Su-25 (NATO code name Frogfoot) is a dedicated subsonic close support aircraft, although other uses have included target towing. Sukhoi initiated work on the aircraft in 1968, a year before an official requirement was announced, allowing the T8 project to be selected for further development just months later. The T8-1 prototype was first flown on 22 February 1975, and in 1980 two other prototypes were sent to Afghanistan for early operational trials. The 200th Independent Attack Air Flight became operational in 1981 and later that year flew missions in Afghanistan.

Production of the **Su-25** ended in 1992, after more than 700 single-seat combat and two-seat training aircraft had been completed, some 210 for export. Many production aircraft each have two non-afterburning Soyuz R-95Sh turbojet engines, each rated at 40.21 kN, although 44.13 kN R-195s went into Su-25BMs and final UBs.

Much care went into survival features, with the pilot occupying a lightweight ejection seat in a cockpit protected by welded titanium plates, plus protected fuel and control systems, a radar warning receiver, chaff/flare dispensers and optional response electronic jammer.

Operational equipment includes Doppler navigation radar, a Klon-PS laser rangefinder/target designator and a photographic camera, while four containers can be carried under the wings to accommodate maintenance equipment to permit extended-period operations away from base.

Su-25T is a further variant (R-195 engines) that first flew on 17 August 1984. This has an improved navigation and attack system to permit use of 'smart' weapons, including the option of 16 laser-beam riding Vikhr anti-tank missiles. The first production **Su-25T** flew in 1990 and it is thought that Russia might have received some 20 Su-25TM variants. Tiny numbers may go to Bulgaria and Slovakia.

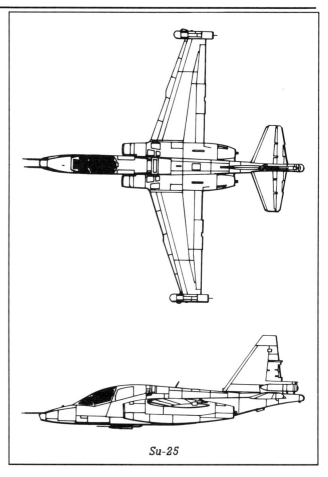

Su-25

Specification

(Su-25)

First prototype: See text
Current users: Afghanistan, Angola, Belarus, Bulgaria, Czech Republic, Georgia, Hungary, Iraq, North Korea, Russia, Slovakia and Ukraine
Crew: Pilot, or two in trainers
Wing span: 14.36 m
Length: 15.53 m
Height: 4.8 m
Max take-off weight: 17,530 kg

Max weapon load: Up to 4,340 kg of attack weapons can be carried on eight pylons under the straight wings, while a further two outboard pylons are dedicated to carrying R-60 (Aphid) air-to-air missiles for self defence. A twin-barrel 30 mm cannon in the fuselage completes the armament.
Maximum speed: Mach 0.82

Service ceiling: 7,000 m
Maximum range: 510 km, or 1,850 km with drop tanks

Su-25. (Piotr Butowski)

Westland Lynx

First flown on 21 March 1971, the **Lynx** formed part of a co-operative helicopter programme between Westland and Aerospatiale of France, with the British company receiving a 70% workshare. A number of versions have been produced within the total of 374 built by July 1995, in both army and naval forms, with naval helicopters operating both from land and ships. Army helicopters can accommodate up to ten troops or cargo and are mainly utility helicopters, although British Mk 7s also undertake anti-tank and support roles.

The principal British Army versions are now the AH Mk 7 and Mk 9, although the majority of the 144 **Lynx** received over the years were of the original AH Mk 1 type, of which many were subsequently upgraded to Mk 7s.

Each Mk 7/9 is powered by two 835 kW Rolls-Royce Gem 42 turboshaft engines driving the BERP advanced four-blade semi-rigid main rotor with swept tips and of composites construction. The Mk 7, as with most army Lynx, has a twin skid undercarriage, while the Mk 9 has wheels. The Mk 9 is very similar to the Battlefield Lynx, the latest export model offered by Westland.

Armament can be eight TOW, HOT or Hellfire anti-tank missiles carried on fuselage outriggers, or alternatively 20 mm cannon pods, two guns pods with two 7.62 mm machine-guns each, or two pods each with ninteen 2.75 in rockets. A pintle-mounted 7.62 mm gun can also be carried in the cabin.

Westland is also studying a conversion package for the army **Lynx** to turn it into a specialised reconnaissance helicopter, incorporating a mast-mounted sight and mission management system. The task for converted helicopters would be to seek out and designate targets for attack helicopters.

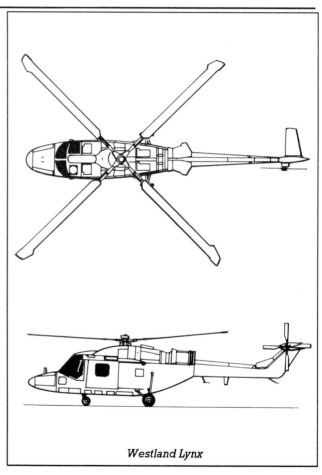

Westland Lynx

Specification

First prototype: See text
Current users: Army versions only:
Norway (for search and rescue),
Qatar (Police) and UK
Crew: Typically one or two
Main rotor diameter: 12.8 m
Length: 15.163 m for AH Mk 7
Height: 3.504 m
Empty weight: 2,577 kg
Max take-off weight: 3,071 kg
Max weapon load: See text
Cruising speed: 259 km/h
Maximum rate of climb: 755 m per
minute
**Hovering ceiling out of ground
effect:** 3,230 m
Maximum range: 631 km

British Army Lynx AH Mk 7 with anti-tank missiles.

Glossary

AAM	Air-to-air missile
AMRAAM	Advanced medium range air to air missile
Avionics	Aeronautical electronics
CFT	Conformal fuel tank
CRT	Cathode ray tube (display)
Drop tank	Detachable auxiliary fuel tank
FLIR	Forward-looking infra-red
'Glass' cockpit.	Electronic display screens replacing conventional instrumentation
HOTAS	Hands on throttle and stick
HUD	Head-up display
IDS	Interdiction/strike
IR	Infra-red
JATO	Jet/rocket assisted take-off
LANTIRN	Low-altitude navigational targeting infra-red for night
Low observable	Stealth
kN	kiloNewton
kW	kiloWatt
MAP	Military Assistance Program
MoU	Memorandum of Understanding
NATO	North Atlantic Treaty Organisation
Pylon	Rigid structure attached to the airframe on which to hang weapons or other stores
RAF	Royal Air Force
SAR	Search and rescue
Ski-jump	Inclined ramp on the deck of an aircraft carrier to allow an aircraft to take-off in a shorter distance or at a heavier weight than would be possible with a flat deck
Stand-off	Remaining at a distance from the target
TIALD	Thermal imaging airborne laser designation
USAF	United States Air Force
USMC	United States Marine Corps
USN	United States Navy